Tender Fires

Other Books by the Authors

Heal My Heart: Pastoral Responses to Sexual and Relational Violence (St. Anthony Messenger Press, 2002)

Your Sexual Self: Pathway to Authentic Intimacy (Ave Maria Press, 1992)

Partnership: Women and Men in Ministry (Ave Maria Press, 1989)

Also by the Authors

Fire Bearers: The Spiritual Qualities of Prophetic Leaders
An Audiocassette (St. Anthony Messenger Press, 2001)

Also by Fran Ferder

Words Made Flesh: Scripture, Psychology, and Human Communication (Ave Maria Press, 1986)

Also by John Heagle

Jesus: Human and Divine (Augsburg Fortress, 1995)

Suffering and Evil: Guidelines for Contemporary Catholics (Thomas More Press, 1987)

On the Way (Thomas More Press, 1981)

Our Journey toward God (Thomas More Press, 1977)

Life to the Full: Reflections on the Search for Christian Fulfillment (Thomas More Press, 1976)

A Contemporary Meditation on Hope (Thomas More Press, 1975)

Tender Fires

The Spiritual Promise of Sexuality

FRAN FERDER
AND
JOHN HEAGLE

A Crossroad Book
The Crossroad Publishing Company
New York

The Crossroad Publishing Company
481 Eighth Avenue, New York, NY 10001

Printed in the United States of America

Library of Congress Cataloging-in-Publication Data

Ferder, Fran.
Tender fires : the spiritual promise of sexuality / Fran Ferder & John Heagle.
p. cm.
Includes bibliographical references.
ISBN 0-8245-1982-5 (alk. paper)
1. Sex–Religious aspects–Catholic Church. 2. Catholic Church–Doctrines. I. Heagle, John. II. Title.
BX1795.S48 F47 2002
241′.66–dc21

2002004078

2 3 4 5 6 7 8 9 10 08 07 06 05 04 03

For the Franciscan Sisters of Perpetual Adoration,
FSPA and AFSPA,
La Crosse, Wisconsin

With gratitude for more than 150 years
of loving presence;
for courage, leadership, and daring vision;
for living the "tender fires" of love and service.

Some day after we have mastered the winds,
the waves, the tides, and gravity,
we will harness for God the energies of love,
and, then, for the second time in the history of the world,
we will have discovered fire.

—Pierre Teilhard de Chardin

Contents

A Personal Word

Why would a nun and a priest write a book about sex? We hear variations of this question whenever we give workshops, teach classes, or publish our work. It is understandably puzzling. What do two celibates have to say about sex that has any significance for people in other lifestyles?

The answer lies both in our professional ministry and our personal lives. It is also related to how one defines "sexuality." As psychotherapists and spiritual counselors for more than twenty-five years, we have come to recognize that whatever initial concerns people bring to counseling, they eventually want to talk about their relationships. Almost everyone seems to struggle with intimacy and human closeness.

Since we believe — and our spiritual tradition proclaims — that sexuality involves relationships that enhance love and life, we have made it a priority to learn as much as we can about intimacy, sexuality, and human loving. In this, our clients, students, and workshop participants have been our best teachers.

On a more personal note, we are both human persons who, though celibate, feel passion, know loss, and experience a deep desire to love and give life. We long for relationships that sustain us. Along with all of God's sons and daughters, we too need to make choices about expressing our sexual energy in ways that fit within the commitments we have made.

Like our clients, our students, and our brothers and sisters everywhere, we have been compelled by our sexuality and challenged by its demands. We have been energized by it, struggled with it, and cried about it. In the end, we have come to recognize that human sexuality embraces everyone in its sacred mysteries. It is a love story that belongs to all of us.

At the outset, we want to acknowledge that our working perspective comes from Roman Catholicism. This is our faith tradition, the horizon of our life experience, and the viewpoint from which we minister and write. At the same time, we hope that these reflections will not only help members of our own faith community, but that they might also offer support to other Christian traditions and anyone who values the sacredness of human relationships. No effort to reach out to a wider community can be carried on in isolation. So, these reflections emerge from our own experience of community and our commitment to dialogue, a desire to listen respectfully to the stories of others who cherish the gift and responsibility of human loving.

A Deep Transformation Is Under Way

When you see a cloud rising in the west, you immediately say, "It is going to rain"; and so it happens. And when you see the south wind blowing, you say "There will be scorching heat"; and it happens. You hypocrites! You know how to interpret the appearance of earth and sky, but why do you not know how to interpret the present time? —Luke 12:54–55[1]

"The search for a healthy relationship is the most important spiritual concern in my life," a professional woman in her thirties told us recently. "It may surprise you to know that my friends and I have long conversations about this. Everyone seems to be struggling to find love in this chaotic world. But where can we turn for guidance? On the one hand, the popular culture tells us to enjoy sex, because it's no big deal—just be safe about it. On the other hand, many church leaders talk about love and then repeat the same familiar warnings and rules. So, the choices are pretty limited. Either we have to settle for one of these two extremes, or sort it out on our own."

This woman is not alone. She and countless other people in our families, workplaces, and churches are trying their best "to sort it out on their own" in the area of sexuality and intimacy. They are looking for love in a conflicted culture. They are struggling to name an experience that reaches beyond our current religious categories, a spiritual quest that is emerging in the midst of our lives and relationships. We believe that she is describing — in simple, poignant words — a profound transformation that is unfolding in our world.

What is the nature of this transformation? In the early 1960s, almost a half century ago, Western culture underwent what came to be known as the "sexual revolution," during which a complex set of events and circumstances unleashed a fresh exploration of human sexuality. It has affected the way we think and talk about marriage and divorce, and introduced us to a whole host of new issues: cohabitation, single parenthood, feminism, gender equality, sexual orientation, relational ethics, and sexuality in the arts and public media.

Some commentators maintain that the sexual revolution of the 1960s and 1970s ended with the onset of AIDS and the rise of other sexually transmitted diseases in the 1980s. In their view the fear of disease and death brought limits to the permissiveness of the previous decades. But this view gives only a shortsighted perspective on a more complex reality. It limits the "revolution" to slogans, statistics, and the visible behaviors — sometimes rebellious and irresponsible — that always accompany times of historical change. Hidden beneath those chaotic beginnings, however, was something far more profound than a passing cultural upheaval or a societal trend. What began stirring almost a half century ago is nothing less than a quiet, dramatic transformation of the very understanding and meaning of human sexuality.

In fact, this "sexual *evolution*" began earlier in the last century. The title of this book is a reference to the prophetic words of Pierre Teilhard de Chardin, a Jesuit priest, paleontologist, and mystic, who concluded an essay on "The Evolution of Chastity" in 1934 with this remarkable observation:

> *Some day after we have mastered the winds, the waves, the tides, and gravity, we will harness for God the energies of love. And, then, for the second time in the history of the world, we will have discovered fire.*

1 Who Will Listen to Our Stories?

Institutions do not make good lovers.
People do.

—Cardinal Danneels

A few years ago, in an ecumenical course that we teach on human sexuality, one of the graduate students asked to speak with us privately after the opening class. Her words came calmly, with the clarity of someone who knew what she wanted to say. "Thank you for approaching sexuality in a positive way and for creating a safe setting for honest dialogue," she began. "I am a divorced, single parent. I love my church and would like to spend my life serving others. But for years now I've felt marginalized and excluded. I understand that religious leaders need to teach about sexuality, but to be honest, it doesn't feel like my life experience matters very much." She paused for a moment and then asked, *"Who will value my story? Who will listen to my voice?"*

This book is the outcome of our ministry of listening. We consider it to be a profound privilege to receive these courageous, often exhilarating, sometimes heartbreaking narratives of people looking for their place at the table of love. We know them as people who take their ethical and personal values seriously and who continue to seek for the self-knowledge and the humility to heal and grow. We also recognize them as people who love their communities of faith and their religious heritage, although some of them are no longer active because they do not feel welcome.

As we begin the twenty-first century, our faith traditions are struggling with the complexities and problems that surround human sexuality. We can be grateful for the nourishment of our sacred writings and traditions, our unfailing source of wisdom and hope. When the Judeo-Christian tradition speaks from its deepest roots about love, mutual respect, the goodness of the body, and the sacredness of relationships, there is no more powerful source of spiritual guidance. But for many people, the urgency surrounding contemporary issues of human sexuality seems greater than what our current religious institutions are able — or at least willing — to address. Many of the cultural, theological, and ethical assumptions of the past are no longer adequate to carry the new century's questions surrounding human relationships. Willing or not, all of us have been plunged headlong into a shared "vision quest" about the meaning and purpose of sexuality and human intimacy.

You might expect your communities of faith to welcome your relationship stories. The opening paragraph of a recent church document describes a community in solidarity with other human pilgrims: "The joys and hopes, the grief and anguish of the people of our time, especially those who are poor and afflicted, are the joys and hopes, the grief and anguish of the followers of Christ as well. *Nothing that is genuinely human fails to find an echo in their hearts.*"[2] Here are the disciples of Jesus as listening communities, people of openness and compassion. We have experienced this listening spirit in parishes, retreat centers, and other small faith communities. We have found it in Protestant congregations and gatherings. We have seen this compassionate stance in many communities of sisters, brothers, and priests. But we recognize — somewhat sadly — that this is not always the case. Our experience over the last decades tells us that many people do not feel safe bringing their search for love, their struggles and failures with relationships to their communities, their pastoral leaders, or other ministers in the churches.

The central question regarding our sexuality is not about our gender, ethnic background, age, vocation, sexual orientation, faith tradition, or even religious and moral convictions, though each of these helps define our uniqueness. But in our heart of hearts — and we believe, in God's eyes — the core issue is not whether we're married or single, divorced or remarried, celibate or sexually active, gay or straight, wounded or well, old or young, male or female. The central question is: *How can I — in the unique circumstances of my life and with God's help and grace — become a more responsible lover and life-giver?* How can I receive the gift of life more reverently and humbly? How can I give life more creatively and joyfully? How can I receive love with more trust and mutuality? How can I give love with more freedom and generosity?

You cannot answer these deeply personal questions with lofty or noble concepts. Your truth cannot be summarized into patterns of moral behavior or reduced to ethical rules. In the end, each of us must discover the meaning of love by carrying it in our hearts and enfleshing it in our relationships. As in Rilke's familiar *Letters to a Young Poet,* we are invited "to love the questions themselves." Each of us must embrace these questions and live them out of our deepest center. There are situations in life where others can "fill in" for us. When you are ill someone else can bring you chicken soup or a casserole. When circumstances prevent you from being at work, a co-worker can take over your responsibilities on the job. But no one else can believe for you, or hope for you, or love for you. No one else can rescue us from the gift or the responsibility of being human. No one else can live our dream or choose our life-project for us. No one else can decide when or with whom we will seek love or how we will express our sexuality.

These reflections invite you to "love the questions" that surround sexuality and intimacy in your life. They are intended to celebrate our shared search to become lovers and life-givers, to encourage growth through self-knowledge, to affirm our ability to become more self-aware and discerning, and to support each of us to find our voice, name our story, and claim the tender fires of human love.

2 Sexual Evolution

The whole creation is standing on tiptoe to see the wonderful sight of the sons [and daughters] of God coming into their own.

—Romans 8:19–20 (Phillips)

At this moment, a child is being born. In this very second, two lovers are running to greet each other, a young man is wondering if he is gay, and an old man is walking behind the coffin of his wife of sixty years. Somewhere, a married couple is reaching orgasm, while another agonizes over how they could have lost a love that once seemed so strong. Right now, a celibate priest is searching the depths of his passion as he prepares a Sunday homily and a single woman is sharing an intimate confidence with a longtime friend. A teenager gazes in the mirror and hopes someone will find her beautiful. A giant gray whale is nursing her calf off the Pacific coast, and a star is bursting forth in a distant galaxy. It is all happening now. It is the sacred energy of sexuality at work and at play in the universe.

Contemplating these images makes it clear that

our contemporary understanding of sexuality is changing. They invite us to expand our way of envisioning sexuality — to stretch the horizon of our experience to welcome its larger meanings.

What is sexuality, and how has our understanding of its mysteries evolved over time? In what ways do sex, sexuality, and love interrelate, and yet remain different? Perhaps even more important to the spiritually aware person, what can help us find greater meaning within the joy and pain of our life's highest experiences: our own stories of loving?

Evolution in Progress

We live in a universe where stars continue to be born in a faraway cosmic nursery. Older ones burn out and disappear. Primal gases dance through the galaxy preparing new planets while earthquakes and volcanoes never stop reshaping our own earth's surface. Evolution, that God-charged thrust toward the future, touches everything. Evolution hones our convictions and refines our cultures. It renews our languages and invites us to consider new ideas. Its constant rhythm of birthing and dying, moving and changing bathes us in energy.

It should not surprise us that sexuality, like all of reality, participates in this dynamic movement. Over the course of its many thousands of years of evolution, the function of sexuality has been slowly shifting from an impersonal procreative instinct to a profoundly intentional expression of love and of life. Once viewed primarily as a built-in way of ensuring the continuation of the species for both animals and humans, sexuality has emerged as a dynamic source of soul communion that includes genital expression and more. As long as human persons have walked upon the earth, they have been struggling to understand this powerful energy and embrace its many gifts. Even before they could articulate the awareness, they were feeling the fire of passion and longing for tenderness.

The Expansive Meaning of Sexuality

Sexuality is a complex word that contains a description of our physical embodiment as male and female persons. It also suggests the fleshy and warm, playful and funny, poignant and sad. At the same time, it is the subject of serious scientific study. The values assigned to sexuality are hotly debated, and cultural differences surrounding it are myriad. "Sexuality" is a word used in describing biological gender, hormonal changes, reproductive realities, social roles, genital conditions, sexual behaviors, physical feelings, gender relations, emotional experiences, intimate relationships, and spiritual commitments.

We draw on the imagery of sexuality in discussing the ecstasy of young lovers, the birth of a baby, and the sacred rituals of cave dwellers. At once playful and serious, expansive yet restrained, the concept of sexuality must allow for the passion of orgasmic release *and* the discipline of responsible choices. It must accommodate the gentle embrace of friends along with the intensity of a lifelong commitment between lovers.

Whether we are chubby babies discovering the pleasure of genital play, little children tending dolls, teenagers swamped in a sea of surging hormones, struggling lovers, lonely widows, mystics in ecstatic union, or ordinary parents caught up in the sometimes chaotic and sometimes wondrous world of family life, we are all immersed in the fragile beauty of our sexuality. Male and female, young and old, gay and straight, whatever our personal lifestyles, educational levels, occupations or spiritual values, we are all sexual — all of the time. Unlike our genital feelings, our *sexuality* does not wax and wane. It is always with us. Its omnipresent energy urges us to connect in some way and on some level to one another — indeed, to all of creation.

3 Transforming the Language of Sexuality

For the sexual language to be sexual, the word must become flesh. —Andre Guindon

In the recent past, the words "sex," "sexuality," and "sexual" have often been used interchangeably, usually with reference to genital realities. The attempt to further delineate them reflects a development in the human experience of loving. With increased emphasis put on the *relational* dimensions of sexuality, our words for it must reflect its evolving meanings.

What is *sex?* Most people today would agree that the words "sex" and "sexuality" are not exactly the same, but they are related. The word "sex," from the Latin *sexus,* is increasingly used as a reference for sexual intercourse, or "having sex"—a use first recorded in the works of D. H. Lawrence in the twentieth century.[3] This recent development illustrates that even our use of terminology in this area is not static. Traditionally, it was thought the word *sexus* was derived from the Latin *secare*, meaning *cut,* and referred to the division or "cutting" of humanity into male and female. This view, which relied on ancient mythology to understand the meaning of gender, is no longer widely held today.[4] Still, the primary use of the word "sex" continues to refer both to sexual intercourse *and* to male and female gender. Sex, in this specific sense, involves all of the wondrous biological capacities and genital characteristics of the human body. It might also be described as the body's gift of sacred pleasures. In fact, popular understanding often equates sex with the physical experience of *erotic energy* — most commonly understood as physical genital pleasure.

What is *sexuality?* Sexuality is love energy. It refers to the spiritual, emotional, physical, psychological, social, and cultural aspects of relating to one another as embodied male and female persons. Sexuality, a still-evolving term, has to do with all the ways we try to reach one another at the level of the heart. It involves our efforts to communicate, our acts of tenderness, and even our struggle to find each other again after an argument. It is the constantly burning fire within us that compels us to turn toward one another. In this sense, we are being sexual — expressing our relational energy as women and men — all of the time. The term "sexuality" is thus more inclusive than the term "sex." One might "have sex" without necessarily sharing much more of the self.

What is *genitality?* A still newer term, "genitality," is increasingly used today to specify biological, physical, or genital sexuality.[5] In some settings, it is gradually replacing the word "sex," which has become confusing with its many layers of meaning. Unlike our sexuality, which is with us always, genitality involves behaviors and feelings confined to a much shorter space of time. While genitality ought to be a very important and vibrant dimension of our sexuality, human experience reveals that genital sharing alone cannot bear all the weight of expressing and maintaining deep human ties. Sexuality cannot be reduced to genitality.

What is the *erotic?* "Erotic" comes from the Greek *eros* (desire). Like most other words that refer to sexual realities, "eros" has been understood in different ways throughout history. Although contemporary Western cultures have tended to reduce it to genital desire, it has traditionally meant love of beauty, longing for goodness, and the soul's restless hunger for God. The tension between eros as a physical drive and eros as a spiritual energy is as old as human memory. Maintaining the "both/and" nature of the erotic has been difficult both for our churches and for individual people. We will address this subject in other parts of the book, but for now, we use the term "erotic" to mean the sacred attraction to beauty and deep desire for fulfillment in all aspects of human life.

4 God's Dream for Sexuality

The Creator intends sexual pleasure for the human creature. —William R. Stayton, Baptist theologian

For believing persons, all creation manifests the holy. As part of the centerpiece of God's creative design, gendered humanity — male and female together — provides an *image* of the God who chose to dwell in flesh. Sexuality is that unique and mysterious vehicle that holds the man and woman together in shared humanity. As such, it is a guardian of God's image. Its essence is sparked with divinity. It has holy intent and sacred meaning. God wants us to be sexual — to be lovers and life-givers. God made us to be passionate — to be capable of feeling the fire of creation within every part of our being. God gave us a large capacity for pleasure of all types.

It is a warm and caring God who placed within us a powerful drive to forge relationships with one another. It is a trusting God, respectful of our freedom, who allows us to discover the mystery of eros as it unfolds in our bodies and our hearts. And it is a playful, pleasure-loving God who gave us smiles and laughter and orgasms, who gave us skin that hungers for touch, who made us desire beauty, and destined us to fall in love. This is the same God who spread diversity over all creation and painted the universe with a palate of colors instead of sixty-four shades of gray. Our human capacity for loving and giving life reflects this diversity and this bright, multicolored reality. The well being of the world rests on our ability to embrace each another in the midst of our differences, to feel empathy, to live as if we are all one flesh.

When we understand the sacred origin of sexuality, we become more attuned to the holy inherent in it. God created sexuality and sexual pleasures in order that human persons might share in their delights in the context of responsibility and care. The fact that this important dimension of God's creation can be used selfishly does not diminish its intrinsic goodness, nor ought it cause us to mistrust our body's gift of pleasures or our soul's delight in human love.

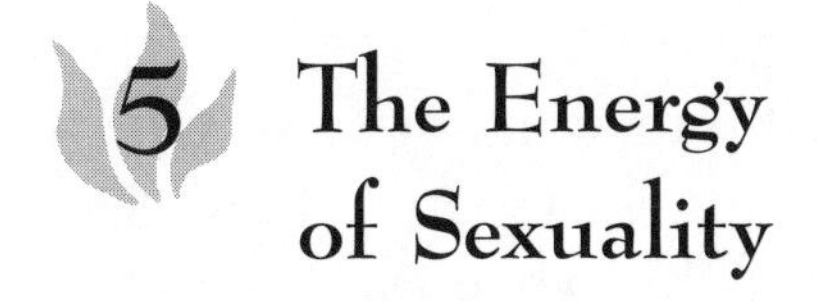

5 The Energy of Sexuality

But one day when I was sitting quiet and feeling like a motherless child, which I was, it come to me: that feeling of being part of everything, not separate at all. I laughed and I cried and I run all around the house. It knew just what it was. In fact, when it happen, you can't miss it. It sort of like you know what, she say, grinning and rubbing me high on my thigh. —Alice Walker

Whenever someone starts an open, inviting conversation about sexuality, new electricity enters the room. The light shines brighter. The air is fresher. Time goes faster. The word itself seems penetrated with little charges of power. Even in people who have had painful encounters with sexuality's potential gifts, we often see a renewed glimmer of hope.

This experience of energy has some scientific basis. Today's cosmologists now know that carbon elements from the original fireball — that first burst of cosmic energy propelling the universe into being — live on in every exchange of human passion, every expression of relational energy, and every display of light in the heavens.[6]

We meet this energy throughout our lives. Whenever friends talk while time waits like a protective sentinel, it is there. On nights when the Milky Way mimics shimmering crystal ornaments in a December sky, its presence is palpable. And each time the sheets are made damp by the sweat of love's most ancient ritual, it is in the air: It is *energy*. It is the primordial fireball pulsing forward in time, bursting into our lives and stirring our hearts with power and passion. It is energy both ancient and new, rooted in a source billions of years old, yet igniting sparks as young as tomorrow.

Any healthy experience of sexuality summons our participation in this energy known by many names: Friendship. Play. Parenting. Mentoring. Making love. Prayer. Each involves a unique interpersonal connection, a sharing of self with another, joining of spirit with spirit. The energy inherent in sexuality tugs at the heart and preoccupies the mind as it invites us into all types of interactions and relationships.

Like any form of energy, it stirs and churns and burns. It will not be quieted until it can express the primordial desire for communion that defines its essence. Not confined to romantic attractions alone, our relationship energy is at work each time we feel our interconnectedness to everything in the cosmos.

It compels our spirit to soar when we stand at the summit of a rugged snow-capped mountain range. It moistens our eyes as we watch a sunrise on a frosty morning in winter. It triggers excitement when we place the last brush stroke on a painting or finish a swimming meet with our best personal time posted on the board.

At times like this, we know we have made contact with an energy that does not belong to us alone. We are quite literally connected to a source of power larger than ourselves. Sometimes quiet, sometimes explosive, this energy fills us with desire, a kind of instinctive yearning for closeness, for connection, for union, for expansion. When we experience its deepest intensity, we recognize our kinship with everyone and everything that calls this universe its home. And our hunger for its ultimate source grows even more intense.

How is this expansive power in the universe specifically related to sexuality? More than a passing physical urge or a gender category, *sexuality* can be even more broadly understood as a unique form of *the energy of attraction that pulsates at the heart of the universe.* Tender enough to communicate non-possessive love, and yet powerful enough to keep the planets from spinning out of control, when this sacred force is directed toward connections that create and sustain life, we call it "sexuality." When it is made conscious in human persons, when it is intentionally directed toward relationships of care, we call it love.[7]

Sexuality Is Energy for Relationship

As human persons all over the world we share the same anatomical structures, the same number of chromosomes, and the same hormones. We are all capable of experiencing many types of pleasure. We all need to be held as infants, and our need for touch continues throughout our lives. Whether we shake hands or bow, kiss or rub noses, we have in common a need for relationship. Much of the activity of our lives across all cultures will be directed toward seeking and sustaining connections with others. We cry when we're hurt, laugh when we're tickled, and eventually fall in love. From Afghanistan to Zimbabwe, our hearts get broken and mended, perhaps many times over.

Yet this cosmos of physiological, emotional, and spiritual unity contains a vast diversity. Our genes might determine our gender, but they don't dictate our values. Our hormones can trigger sexual arousal, but they don't decide universal sexual absolutes. Our similarities drive us toward one another even while our differences may make us enemies. At the heart of this complex and often volatile diversity, the energy eager for connection, indeed communion, can be described as *energy for relationship*. It will continually turn us toward one another. It can be counted upon to awaken, in each new generation, a body/soul desire for communion as unquenchable as the fire that gave it life.

As a human community, we have tended to view sexuality as an isolated drive with a particular set of functions. We have been less aware of its relationship to other energies in the universe. Thus, this remarkable power to forge interpersonal connection has not been understood as *connected* to anything beyond itself — a fact that may have influenced how our expressions of sexuality often drift away from their inherent purpose — to make relationship their home.

The Limits of New Descriptions

How far can we go? When does expanding the concept imperil its meaning for human relationships? Are the stars in a distant constellation really continuous with the light in our eyes when we see our beloved? Doesn't the uniqueness of a friendship lose something distinctly human when compared to ocean mammals and carbon molecules in outer space? Any word can lose its meaning when it has been made so inclusive that it no longer delineates a specific reality.

Clearly, one of the challenges today is how to

broaden the meaning of sexuality, to incorporate its wider nuances and root it in its primordial source, without losing its connection to reproduction, sexual behavior, and male-female gender. We don't want to make it carry more than it can. Instead, we hope to articulate an awareness of the deeper meaning already in it. Human sexuality is *energy for relationship.* But sexuality is not the only form of energy that exists—rather, it is part of a larger spectrum of energy. The new physics now understands all energies to be related, part of a great whole with different manifestations and expressions. "All of the power of the big bang is in us, the God of the galaxies is within us. . . ."[8] Out of this larger spectrum, this primal field of fire, human sexual energy finds its origins. When human persons love one another they are stepping into the energy field where little universes of fire are ignited, where chemistry occurs, where something within them will be set aflame. When they caress their young, honor the confidence of a friend, make sacrifices for those in need—and, in the words of Neil Diamond, "weep when it is all done for being done too soon"—they are entering more deeply into the heart of the galaxy. In so doing, they are truly communing with the divine. The early mystics who saw a connection between sexuality and fire were not simply employing metaphor—they were in touch with a mystery not yet articulated at their own time in history.

6 Can Sex Be Separated from Sexuality?

Every sensuous experience is at heart a spiritual one: a divine revelation. —David Steindl-Rast

We occasionally meet people who say: "We have sex but it's just a physical thing. Neither one of us is ready for anything more serious so we're not going to get emotionally involved." How possible is this really? How long can two people come together genitally, enjoy mutual pleasure, and keep their feelings out of it? While their bodies become one, can their hearts remain detached? Having an orgasm under these circumstances is certainly possible, but sooner or later healthy individuals will develop feelings of connection. Physical vulnerability eventually exposes the soul and arouses the heart as well as the body.

Here's where *sexuality* reveals itself as more than *genitality*. Sexuality involves the whole person. Its voice calls out for communion from every fiber of our being. It won't be silenced while our genitals enjoy a few moments of disconnected pleasure. As *energy for relationship*, sexuality will not allow our feelings to stand on the sidelines while our bodies seek human closeness without them. If it senses union happening anywhere, sexuality quickly summons our hearts.

While sexuality is clearly a *body energy* with strong physical sensation, it cannot be confined to flesh. At the same time, it is a powerful force for emotional and spiritual union housed in a physical body. Experienced *both* in our bodies and in our souls — it can be named an orgasm, a mystical union, or a manifestation of a close relationship. We cannot separate its many facets without doing real damage to ourselves, and to the community of brothers and sisters who depend on us to live out of the energy of the Great Commandment. Perhaps one of the greatest challenges for our societies and our church communities is to maintain the *both/and* dimensions of sexuality: It is *both* physical *and* spiritual. It is *both* wounded *and* good.

7 Sexuality and Spirituality: A Sacred Friendship

This is my commandment: love one another.

—John 15:12 (JB)

We have described sexuality as *energy for relationship*—as a uniquely human form of participation in the sacred fire of the universe that directs us toward love. But what is spirituality? How is it related to sexuality? The word itself has complex and ancient roots. Its more popular usage refers to those things that have to do specifically with God, or with one's relationship to the holy. Often, the word "spiritual" has been used in contrast with the words "secular" or "material" to separate what is truly "of God" from what supposedly has no business in the realm of the divine. The body/soul dualism is part of that separation—one that has perpetuated a belief that God prefers disembodied souls to the sweaty, sticky, fleeting world of flesh.

However, when we emphasize the interconnectedness of all things, it's much harder to enforce sharp divisions between the secular and the sacred, or the material and the spiritual. Rather, emerging cosmology sees the physical world as a manifestation of divine reality. Since all things participate in the great spectrum of God's creation, all things *have spirit*— a unique *within* or particular *inwardness* that houses their identities. Spirituality doesn't oppose physicality. Rather, spirituality is the deepest aspect of all things. According to this view of spirituality, a rock has spirit. A piece of wood has a "within." Both reflect, in their individual uniqueness, a deep inward spark of divinely created reality. God is not indifferent to trees.

In the human person, that spiritual "within" is often called "soul" — the center of consciousness. Soul shelters individuality and gives us space for awareness and reflection. Together, body and soul represent different vantage points of your unique reality — a reality that is a continuous and inseparable sacred whole. In this way, blood and bone, muscle and skin are sacred. They are constantly involved in a great silent dialogue, an inner symphony of soul communion. Though most of us may not be used to thinking of our sexual parts in this way, they too are sacred. They have both a "without" and a "within" — a physical manifestation and a deep inner connection to our capacity for reflective awareness. Put another way, they too participate in "soul." Continuous with our deepest identity, they whisper messages to our heads and our hearts. They form part of the great communication pathway along which love travels and the energies of connection play.

If sexuality is energy for relationship, spirituality is its guide. Sexuality and spirituality are soul sisters that share the same energy source. They belong together. Spirituality without sexuality is a phantom — a ghost of piety with a hollow center. When spirituality loses its grounding in relational energy, it grows cold and unfeeling. Sexuality without spirituality is equally empty — it is literally *without spirit.* Disconnected from awareness, spiritless attempts to form relationships lack depth and meaning.

As Christians, we have to struggle continually for a more liberating vision of human sexuality and support the natural connection between sexuality and spirituality. We have to heal our tendency to make them enemies and allow a friendship to flourish between them. In so doing, we will see that anything authentically and deeply human is inherently spiritual. To love is our desire and our destiny. And it is on this journey toward embodied love that our spirituality will find its best home.

8 Longing for Intimacy

All the lonely people,
where do they all come from?

—The Beatles

Is There Enough Love?

Wisdom lies not only in knowledge, but also in asking the right questions. Recently, a religious educator invited us to speak to her youth group on the meaning of faith, hope, and charity. After we introduced the topic, we invited the young adults to share their own convictions about believing, hoping, and loving. After a long silence, a wise young student raised her hand.

"To tell you the truth," she began, "we probably are a bit cynical about topics like this. Our social studies teacher tells us that our political institutions are in crisis and that we will continue to face global terrorism for decades. Our science instructor tells us that there is a hole in the ozone layer and that hundreds of species are dying every year. It's difficult to talk about faith and hope in this kind of a world. And as for loving, I would like to ask you a question. *Do you think there is enough love left in the world to hold it together?*"

She paused long enough to glance at her classmates and then went on: "I know there isn't enough love in my family, and it doesn't feel like there's enough love in this school. I don't think there is enough love in this town or in this country. But sometimes, late at night when I'm trying to pray, I think there must be enough love somewhere."

This young woman would probably not consider herself a theologian, but she raised a significant theological question. At one time or another, her question has probably bothered each of us. It stirs silently in our hearts as we struggle with stress in our lives and tensions in our relationships. We feel it tug at our consciousness when we watch the evening news. We see it mirrored in the eyes of refugees fleeing from genocide, famine, and disease.

For many of us the question is more immediate and personal: Is there enough love in my life to keep me going from day to day? Is there enough connection so that I don't feel isolated and alone? Is there enough understanding, enough compassion to find meaning? How can I heal from the betrayals of love in my life, the collapse of trust? How can I find the gift of authentic intimacy? This young woman's question needs to be taken seriously, since it reflects the quiet concerns of so many people in our families, our workplaces, and our society.

Too Stressed for Intimacy

Why does human loving appear to be so hard in our contemporary life? For one thing, we live such busy, harried lives that we have little time for those things that truly nourish the human spirit. Most of us spend our lives figuratively if not literally "on the run" scrambling to get to work on time, grabbing a quick lunch, picking up the children from soccer, fighting rush-hour traffic to get home, collapsing in front of the TV. As a society we suffer from a kind of psychic and emotional jet lag: we never quite catch up to ourselves.

A few years ago newspaper headlines announced the results of a study regarding sexual behavior in the United States. Those who conducted the study were "stunned" by the high percentage of both women and men who were disappointed by their personal experience of sex. As psychotherapists we found that the study simply confirmed much of our everyday clinical experience. If anything, we were surprised by the experts' surprise.

Our stress-filled lifestyle has an inevitable impact on our relationships. Studies have shown that the average American household spends only eight to twelve minutes a day in face-to-face verbal contact. Moreover, most of these daily conversations are what theorists describe as only "first-" or "second-level" communication, involving the exchange of pleasantries, schedules, and other practical information. In many people's lives deeper forms of self-disclosure are minimal or almost nonexistent. We're thus trying to conduct relationships in a culture that doesn't particularly value interpersonal communication.

This lack of authentic intimacy is literally killing us. Our physical health suffers from touch deprivation, whether this includes the simple expressions of daily affection, the comfort and reassurance of a hug, or the tender caress of a loved one's hand. Our lack of intimacy is also crippling our emotional and spiritual lives. When there isn't time for quiet conversations and shared stories, sexual intercourse is missing the language of the heart. Without the background music of mutuality and tenderness, it can easily become one more task to perform, one more test to pass, a masquerade for authentic intimacy.

The Challenge of Cyber Relations

If the ability to share information were the secret of success, our tiny planet should be one of the most gregariously happy places in the Milky Way. We are surrounded by the whirring, buzzing, blinking, and beeping of cell phones, satellite dishes, personal computers, copiers, faxes, and modems. Whether we are awake or asleep, the headline stories are updated every fifteen minutes and somewhere the financial markets are open. There are many gifted dimensions to this emerging world of communication technology. Like other extensions of our bodies and our brains, these tools can serve as instruments of understanding, respect, and the advancement of the human adventure.

The paradox is that as the world grows smaller through communication advances, its people seem to be more relationally volatile and potentially fragmented. Even as the Web becomes more sophisticated and encompassing, the potential for anonymity, isolation, and alienation also increases. Perhaps more than ever before in history the human heart cries out for real contact with other people. Not just the virtual reality of images or the flood of data, but the flesh-and-blood world of friends and lovers — a world where we reach for another's person's hand in the night, see the tender gaze in another's eyes, or taste the salty tears on another's cheeks.

We have, as a society, become more litigious, adversarial, and cynical. We are less courteous and more aggressive. We don't dialogue, compromise, or arbitrate; we sue! We are more likely to demand our rights than we are to listen to the perspective or the needs of others. We suffer from road rage, psychic overload, and spiritual emptiness.

In her book *The Argument Culture* Deborah Tannen describes the ways in which the media and our education system engender debate instead of dialogue.[9] News stories emphasize sensationalism, violence, and drama, and the lyrics of contemporary music often employ violent, oppressive rhetoric in speaking of women and sexuality. TV approaches the political process by casting it in terms of battle plans, strategies, and frontlines. Communication workshops for managers and corporations are not as much about genuine listening or verbal clarity as they are about learning aggressive techniques of exploitation and psychic manipulation.

These culturally approved adversarial attitudes have an impact on our day-to-day relationships with co-workers, close friends, and family members. In a world where psychic aggression is chic, and image counts more than substance, it's not easy to be vulnerable to another person without being dismissed as weak. When we are continually told to assert our own rights, it is risky to acknowledge our personal failures—to say: "I'm sorry." In a society that thrives on competition, it requires courage to reach out a hand in reconciliation or to take the initiative in healing old hurts.

9 There *Is* Hope for Our Loving

Acquire a heart and you shall be saved.

—Abba Pambo, desert father

In the early decades of Christian history, a spiritual leader reminded the members of his community to "cling to the Lord in your hearts, and always be prepared to give the reasons for your hope" (1 Pt 3:15, our translation). We've listened to the honest questions that concern people seeking compassion and caring in this demanding world. We've named some of the major obstacles to authentic intimacy and life-giving sexuality in our culture. So, where can we look for encouragement and support?

In his book *The Prophetic Imagination* Walter Brueggemann points out that authentic renewal demands not only that we *criticize with courage,* but that we also *energize with hope.*[10] It is not enough to just say "no" to sexual and relational values that differ from our own. We must also explore and claim what we want to say "yes" to in our journey toward

GETTING SMART ABOUT RELATIONSHIPS

Recently, Mark, a successful manager came to our center to begin counseling. He spoke of how hard he had studied to live up to his parents' expectations and achieve a consistently high grade point average in high school. He had won a scholarship to a respected university, majored in engineering, graduated with honors, and was offered a high-paying position. Within a few years he married, had two children, and rose through the ranks of his company into positions of leadership. He took his career and his faith seriously. He attended church every Sunday and was active in the civic community. In the eyes of the world, Mark had achieved it all. What most people didn't know was that he was painfully shy and felt anxious in most social situations. His colleagues weren't aware that he suffered from a lack of intimacy in his life, that he wrestled with depression and feelings of failure, or that he was, for most part, unable to share his feelings, and that his marriage of sixteen years was all but over.

As his first session was about to end, Mark looked out the window for a moment, and then said, "I've spent all these years doing what I thought a good husband and father was supposed to do, but now I'm becoming aware that my wife and my children don't really know me, and I don't know them. Not in any really close way. It feels like I have to go back somewhere and start learning about life all over again."

Many people's stories parallel Mark's. Our culture invests most of its resources in IQ — the "intelligence quotient" — that it takes to run computers, corporations, and commerce, but we don't place the same value on EQ[11] — "emotional intelligence" — the ability to communicate effectively and lovingly with those with whom we live and work. Our nation spends billions of dollars improving SAT scores in science, mathematics, and computer technology. These are often necessary and helpful investments. But we don't provide similar resources to help our citizens grow in the skills of human communication and intimacy: listening, self-disclosure, conflict management, to name only a few. It is often people most successful with their mental gifts who experience aching voids in their emotional lives. This imbalance is creating a crisis of relationships, a potential breakdown of our ability to understand and listen to one another.

deeper human communion. Here are two compelling reasons to believe in the resilient goodness of love.

The Longing for Love

God has created each of us to be sacraments of the sacred, icons of the divine. And the central mystery of God — the heart of the holy — is *communion.* This thirst for love and this longing for connection is woven into the very fabric of our "inmost self." This longing is like a pilot light that doesn't go out, a yearning that will not die. This is the first and most abiding reason for our hope: that the hunger for intimacy will always be greater than the fear of its consequences.

We are created for communion. We are made to belong. It is the ache that stirs in us when we are separated from those we love or when we can't fall asleep at three o'clock in the morning. It is the pang of loneliness that comes when we hug a friend good-bye at the airport or escort our elderly parents on to the train on their way home after the holidays. It is the indescribable feeling of longing that comes in late autumn, at the turning of the year, as we watch the last maple leaves fall to the ground and the sun move low on the horizon. It is the tears that well up in our eyes when we have a foolish, painful quarrel with our beloved and can't find the words or even the effort to reach out in reconciliation.

Most of us have known the sudden and perplexing onset of loneliness in the midst of a crowd of people, at a party, or leaving the theater after watching a film. These everyday encounters with loneliness remind us of our longing for communion. They come as a silent memo, a wakeup call from the heart, the spirit's sonar echoing from somewhere in our depths. Loneliness is an integral dimension of the human condition, a quiet reminder that we are creatures — limited, mortal, unfinished, and radically interdependent. It would be sad if we awoke one morning and came to our kitchen only to discover that there was no food. But it would be far more tragic if we awoke one morning and discovered that we were no longer hungry. The longing for love, the ache for relationships, is God's primal beatitude, the first and most lasting blessing of our lives.

What Really Goes On Behind Closed Doors?

Most people, young and old, value the goodness and grounding of genuine mutuality in their lives. They sincerely seek the encouragement, the resources, and the tools to grow in their skills of communication and intimacy. Sometimes we have to look beyond popular cultural images to discover these stabilizing concerns and values. For instance, the financial success of the film industry tells us that many Americans go regularly to movies with strong sexual content. Viewer surveys also indicate that we spend a lot of time watching TV sitcoms that offer frank—and often boring—conversations about the sexual exploits of their protagonists.

At the same time, on a more personal level, we tend to be surprisingly serious about faithfulness and authentic intimacy. We may browse through the tabloids as we stand in line at the supermarket, but more of us want to learn how to be closer to those we love than really relish reading about the exotic and often tragic stories of others. One of the surprising discoveries in the landmark study *Sex in America* is that despite their vicarious interest in casual sex and promiscuity, a large percentage of married Americans want stability in their relationships, and the majority of them actually choose monogamy and fidelity to their commitments.[12]

There are other signs of hope as well. Though it is still alarmingly high, the rate of divorce in this country has begun to level off. Most churches take seriously the responsibility of preparing couples for marriage. Many religious groups offer support networks for gay and lesbian persons. National statistics indicate that the number of teenage pregnancies is lower, as is the percentage of violent crime and rape. The meaning and implications of these statistics depend on our perspective and moral agenda. The fact remains, however, that there are positive indicators of a quiet, emerging sense of sexual and relational responsibility. The number of people who seek support of various kinds — including small groups related to communication and intimacy, emotional and spiritual healing, continues to grow in this country. This is the second reason to hope: people are searching for authentic intimacy in their relationships and appear more willing to invest time and energy to make it happen.

10 Holy Belonging

We do not die from the darkness.
We die from the cold.

—Miguel de Unamuno

As our wise student asked in an earlier chapter, Is there enough love left in the world to hold it together? On our more hopeful days as believers, we want to say yes, there is enough love. There is potentially enough love in our families, in our schools, in our offices, hospitals, and shopping malls. God has given us an abundance of this gift, the overwhelming love poured out into our lives and communities. On the level of belief, we can say *yes*. But, as we know all too well, doctrine is not necessarily mirrored in life. It is a broken and sometimes cynical world that we journey in, and our ideals are not necessarily reflected in our practice. Like the world around us, our promise is usually better than our performance.

This leaves us with important choices to make. We can acknowledge our culture's superficialities and the obstacles it puts in the way of responsible relationships, and still claim for ourselves a more powerful and transforming vision. "Do not be conformed to this age," Paul writes to his fellow Christians in Rome, "but be transformed by the inner renewal of your minds" (Rm 12:1, JB). We can recognize our society's exploitative values without withdrawing from it in self-righteousness or rejecting our brothers and sisters with whom we share its burdens and possibilities. Similarly, we can acknowledge our own blindness and brokenness, our inability — or at times, our unwillingness — to love, and still respect the desire for communion and the willingness to pursue it.

Sometimes it is precisely in our emptiness and alienation that our wounded hearts recognize both the need and possibility of God's graciousness. In his novel *Life after God* Douglas Coupland gives us, in the poignant musings of his main character, a profile of a heart wounded by disillusionment but open to the healing grace of God:

> *Now — here is my secret:*
>
> *I tell it to you with an openness of heart that I doubt I shall ever achieve again, so I pray that you are in a quiet room as you hear these words. My secret is that I need God — that I am sick and can no longer make it alone. I need God to help me give, because I no longer seem*

RECLAIMING OUR ROOTS

In our ministry, we often meet people who tell us that they are "spiritual" in their values, but no longer belong to an "organized religion." Many of them believe, rightly or wrongly, that institutional religion is too preoccupied with externals, rules, and ethical control. "The official church keeps giving answers to questions that few people are asking," a young medical intern told us, and then added, "it just doesn't seem to have a relevant message for today." While we can understand these criticisms, we grieve that many of these sincere persons are not aware of the powerful vision grounding our traditions. Perhaps the most challenging task — for both religious institutions and spiritual seekers — is that of reclaiming the wisdom of our heritage. The creation stories in Genesis (chapters 1–2:4 and 2:5–3:24) are an integral part of this grounding vision, for they provide us with an affirming and insightful understanding of God's creative intentions for sexuality, as well as a realistic description of the human condition. We cannot underestimate the practical wisdom conveyed in these narratives, since they form the basis for the entire Judeo-Christian posture toward human relationships and the meaning and purpose of sexuality. Both stories affirm that:

- God is the source and creator of our world and relationships.
- Creation is inherently good.
- Women and men are created as equal partners in the image of God.
- Human beings are called "to till and to keep" the earth.
- Women and men are morally responsible and accountable to God and to one another.
- Human sexuality is the culminating high point of the creative process.
- Every human being is called to be a lover and a life-giver.
- Creation and human life are gifted but limited realities.
- The open-ended nature of human consciousness brings us face to face with the mystery of freedom — where we find the possibility of choosing good or evil.

capable of giving; to help me be kind, as I no longer seem capable of kindness; to help me love, as I seem beyond being able to love.[13]

The secret of each of our hearts is that we need God. We need the gift of grace to integrate our sexual energy and to learn to love respectfully and well. The secret of our lives is that we also need one another; that through our relationships we encounter the face of God. The secret of hope is that love and graciousness are available to us personally and communally through our willingness to walk in trust.

In his letter to the Colossians, Paul employs a striking metaphor that illumines this chapter's opening question. He tells us that the risen Christ exists before all things, "and in him all things *hold* together" (Col 1:17, emphasis ours). In the end, the attitudes and behaviors that wound us and break our hearts are not as strong as the love that can hold us together. The forces that fragment our relationships are not as powerful as the healing presence that can make us whole.

11 The Goodness of Human Passion

Let him kiss me with the kisses of his mouth! For your love is better than wine, your anointing oils are fragrant, your name is perfume poured out. —Song of Songs 1:2–3

For thousands of years the book often called the Song of Songs has been a source of fascination, affirmation, joy, and — for some at least — considerable puzzlement and dismay. Many of the ancient Jewish rabbis, the early church fathers, and not a few contemporary believers have wondered how this collection of erotic love poetry entered the canon of the sacred writings of Israel and Christianity.

How are we to understand the open and frank celebration of physical beauty, passion, and sensual pleasure that we find in this collection of poems? Whatever interpretive approach we take to this book, there is near unanimous agreement that it contains a strong affirmation of human love.

The sensuous poetry of the Song of Songs strikes remarkable parallels and contrasts with the story of Adam and Eve. The setting is once again in a garden and the Eden-like surroundings return us to an atmosphere of harmony, beauty, and delight. It's as though the disaster of disobedience and the consequent fracturing of relationships has never happened. Or it's only a distant memory, a spiritual wound that God's gracious love has healed and restored. The human couple is at home in their surroundings and equally at ease with their bodies, emotions, and feelings. They are once again "naked and without shame." The human senses have regained their capacity for enjoyment and are in the service of mutuality and love. Plants and animals surround the couple in a playful dance of harmony and delight. The description of the relationship between the Shulamite woman and her soul-mate transcend the conventional gender roles of that era.

The male is not dominant in stereotypical fashion, nor is the female subordinate physically and emotionally. In the rich tapestry of these verses, this industrious and independent woman tends her vineyards and pastures her flocks. She is fully the equal of the man. The man, on the other hand, is portrayed as tender, receptive, and able to convey his

WHY IS LOVE SO DIFFICULT?

Several years ago a couple that had been married for more than thirty years came to our center for marital therapy. When they began counseling, their relationship was at the breaking point, but they tried to set aside their bitter memories and patterns of avoidance and anger, and committed themselves to learn better ways of communicating. After nearly a year of difficult, honest conversations, they began to see glimmers of hope. One afternoon, as they were leaving after a particularly difficult session, the husband — a quiet, reflective man — turned to us and said, "If love and sexuality are supposed to be good, then why is this so painful and difficult?"

This man's question articulates a larger human quest — the search for a compelling and comprehensive understanding of love. What can our spiritual roots tell us about learning to love? Is sexuality really a gift? Or is it only a seductive decoy for pain and grief? Why *are* human relationships so difficult?

Intimacy is at once an experience that our hearts long for *and* a journey that we fear. It is both gift and burden. We hear it as the siren song of romantic union, but resist it as a trek into the perilous terrain of risk and vulnerability. Like our search for God, our encounter with human love is a mystery that fascinates and terrifies us, invites and intimidates us.

feelings of desire and love. He seeks out and occasionally approaches the woman, but more often she initiates their meetings. Her choices and movements are bold and open. She speaks of her beloved with unabashed passion to her women friends and seeks him out in the streets and squares of the city.

In short, this is a portrait of mutuality, a celebration of human loving and passion that honors both the sensuousness of physical love and its spirit of reverent mutuality. The images and themes outlined here have a perennial relevance and are capable of evoking the longing for love in every age and heart. The popular media and images of contemporary culture perpetuate the assumption that in order for someone to have "good sex," it must be "naughty" — in a context outside of an exclusive, permanent commitment. Commitment supposedly takes the "fun" out of sex. The poet-author of the Song of Songs certainly doesn't see life and relationships this way! The love between this woman and man is passionate, celebratory, joyful, and sensuous; but it is also committed, faithful, monogamous, and covenantal.

The Vulnerability of Loving

The evident faithfulness and commitment leads us to another central theme in this book: the experience of absence and unfulfilled longing. The Song of Songs is not about some primeval world without struggle, sacrifice, or suffering. It's not a utopian garden free of loss or absence or a blissful island of romance without responsibility. The two lovers long for each other's presence and seek each other in the night. But do they ever fulfill their longing? Do they finally consummate their union? The ongoing dialogue is inconclusive and perhaps deliberately ambivalent. The couple's seeking and finding, their comings and goings seem dreamlike. They appear to find each other only to slip away again, to rejoice in communion and then to ache with absence. Perhaps the poetry and its extravagant metaphors are as much about the vulnerability of love and human passion as they are about fulfillment and the ecstasy of union.[14]

A Love Stronger Than Death

The biblical vision of human love both reassures and challenges us. What are some practical spiritual lessons that we might learn from this ecstatic wisdom? How does the Song of Songs speak to our lives and relationships? The soaring joy of love has no equal in human experience. It can bless us with greater joy and fulfillment and expand our sense of well-being, whether we undertake the adventure of falling in love, experience the intense passion of sexual intercourse, or enjoy the quiet bond of enduring celibate friendship. On the other hand, there is probably no dimension of our lives that can bring us more desolation and rejection, more shame and emotional despair, than love that fails or relationships that fall apart. Whether we can find the words for it or not, we all know, somewhere inside of us, this paradox of sexuality and love. "I've looked at love from both sides now," the words of Joni Mitchell's song remind us, "From up and down, and still somehow, it's love's illusions I recall. I really don't know love at all." Who of us can say that we really understand love? Who has fully comprehended its pain or its promise?

Perhaps the most important lesson from the Song of Songs is that of love's mystery and goodness in the midst of struggle. Diversity *and* unity, differentiation *and* mutuality, are integral to God's dream for the universe. The call to partnership between woman and man is God's creative intention, and even though that companionship is bruised and wounded by human exploitation, God promises healing for relationships and redemption for our fractured intimacy. No matter how risky human intimacy may appear to be, it still leads to deeper life and fulfillment. No amount of human selfishness or oppression can obliterate the image of God at the center of every sunrise and smiling face. What God created in the divine image and saw as very good continues to be a source of grace and communion. "Love," the Song of Songs reminds us, "is strong as death; . . . many waters cannot quench love, neither can floods drown it" (Sg 8:6–7).

12 Our God Puts on Skin

And the Word became flesh,
and lived among us.

—John 1:14

We met Cindy when she was considering a change in her career. At that time, she was a single parent and a kindergarten teacher who wanted to return to graduate school and prepare for full-time ministry in the church. At a workshop on relationships, she shared an engaging story about her son, Jeremy, who was four years old. One evening she invited a couple of her closest friends to her apartment for dinner. After they had eaten, she put Jeremy to bed with the hope that she and her friends would have some time to visit. Within minutes the youngster reappeared in the living room and announced that he was thirsty. Cindy gave him a drink of water and tucked him in again, only to have him reappear shortly because he had to go to the bathroom.

Patiently, but a bit exasperated, Cindy put him back in bed, stroked his forehead, and said, "Jeremy,

I know you want to be where the excitement is, but it's past your bedtime, so I really want you to stay here and go to sleep. Will you please do that for Mommy?"

Jeremy replied, "But, Mom, I can't stay here. I'm afraid of the dark."

"Now, Jeremy," his mother began, "you know that you're not usually afraid of the dark. And besides, there's no reason to be afraid — God is right here with you."

Jeremy thought quietly for a moment. Then, with a furrow in his brow, he said, "Oh, I know God is here, Mom. But I want somebody in here with skin on!"

Living in Our Skin

Clearly, Jeremy is both a skilled negotiator and, in his own way, a remarkably wise young theologian. He may have been stretching his imagination — and his mother's patience — in his search for excuses to stay up, but in the process he named an important truth about the human condition. We all want to have someone in our lives "with skin on" — a real flesh-and-blood human presence acquainted with thirst and hunger; someone who recognizes our need to stay up late and "be where the excitement is." We need someone who understands our experience from the inside, who knows how good it feels to watch the sunrise on a clear morning or to dive into a clear lake on a hot August afternoon; someone who knows the emptiness of loss, the ache of a fever, the comfort of home cooking, and the warmth of human touch.

The truth is that Jeremy, with his child's wisdom, described the central vision of our Christian faith. We belong to an *incarnational* religion. We believe that it is an inherent quality of every human being to be em-bodied — to be wrapped around, immersed in, and gifted by skin. With this gift comes the sensations of touch, the vulnerability to pain and the mystery of arousal, the wonder of our emotions and feelings. Our spirituality tells us to look for God, not in the abstract or in some ethereal world, but in the earthiness of creation.

We grow up and mature into life in our bodies and with the other bodies in our circle of relationships, including the all-encompassing "body" of the earth. The seasons of our lives are immersed in the rich landscape of morning glories and wild rivers, of mountains and rolling wheat country; of verdant fields of alfalfa, corn, and oats; of rugged coastlines, Douglas firs, and the eye-pleasing contours of the land, sea, sky. We encounter the holy in the arms that hold us as infants and the hands that guide our first steps; in the jostling physicality of childhood play; in the friendship of our classmates; in the ache of our first love; in the faces of our friends and in the eyes of those whose caring mirrors our own intense feelings of connection. We know something about the mystery of God through the en-fleshed presence of other human beings — in their smiles and frowns, in their hands and voices, in their flesh and sinew, and the flowing music of their emotions.

God in the Flesh

An incarnational spirituality emerges from God's inner life, as that mystery has been manifested and enfleshed in creation and the history of salvation. As Christian disciples we understand human sexuality as flowing from the Triune God's life of generativity and love, and this unity-in-diversity shows itself in the splendor of an evolving universe, in the incarnation of the eternal Word, in the outpouring of the Spirit on humanity, and in the faces, eyes, and loving touch of our sisters and brothers. "Christ plays in ten thousand places," writes Gerard Manley Hopkins in his poem "Inversnaid," "lovely in limbs, and lovely in eyes not his."

Contemporary theologians have helped us reclaim a spirituality that is rooted in the ever-present mystery of God.[15] Their revitalized understanding of Trinitarian theology offers divine life as a model for all human relationships. As Christians our lives are not focused on solitary salvation or a self-absorbed spirituality. Rather, we are invited and then reinvited to participate in communion with God and others. We are created to be in community. We are called to mirror the mysterious dynamic of diversity, equality, mutuality, uniqueness, and interdependence in God's complexity.

The consequences of this vision are momentous. God isn't a distant divinity dwelling somewhere beyond the far reaches of the universe. Ours is a God whose life is inherently generative, revealing, and communal. The incarnation of the eternal Word in Jesus, the sacred character of all creation, and our own bodily selves — all of these overflow the banks of a generous love, the self-expression of God's inner communion.

When we Christians speak of the incarnation, we are most often referring to the central belief of our faith tradition — that the eternal Word of God became flesh in Jesus of Nazareth, and that in his life, his ministry, his suffering, dying, and rising, he healed and transformed the human experience into a holy path toward life.

The life and person of Jesus is certainly the most striking instance of the en-fleshment of God in the midst of human life. The Jewish tradition into which Jesus was born revered the earthy goodness of "being in the flesh." It viewed the human person not in the divided, dualistic manner that is familiar to us in many Western cultures, but as a unified being—an animated body, an integrally enfleshed spirit. Nor did the Hebrew vision have a comfortable belief in a purely spiritual afterlife. Either God would raise up the whole bodily person or there would be only the shadowy, lifeless world of Sheol.

Unlike the Greek philosophical outlook that influenced later Judaism and early Christianity, the prophetic and wisdom literature take seriously the created world as a reflection of God's presence and creativity. The fullness of life for a Jewish person was a life of *shalom* — an earthy celebration of sensuousness, human love, children, food, wine, and the abundance of the earth. The prophets did not view heaven or the reign of God as an escape from the "illusions of the earth," but as a great banquet, hosted by God, involving peace and harmony among the people of the earth, a celebration in which the "mountains will run with new wine and the hills all flow with it" (Amos 9:13, JB).

This is clearly not the same world the neo-Platonists envisioned, which later influenced early Christian writers such as Augustine. In an ironic play on words, Plato taught that the *soma* (the body) is a *sema* (a prison), from which we must escape through our pursuit of true knowledge and the eternal forms. In the Judeo-Christian tradition the body is not a prison; it is a gift—albeit a precarious gift—

a vibrant way of being in the world and relating to other human beings.

We can see this contrast in the different ways Socrates and Jesus faced their deaths. Socrates, condemned to drink the hemlock, serenely told his friends and followers not to be sad or to weep, because his death would enable him to leave this illusory world for the real world of the spirit. In contrast, when Jesus faced his suffering and death, he gathered "his own," washed their feet in a gesture of loving service, and asked them to remember him in the breaking of the bread and the sharing of the cup. At Gethsemani he asked his closest followers to stay awake with him for strength and comfort. Jesus then entered into agony of spirit and begged God to "let this chalice pass me by." As a true son of Abraham and Sarah, Jesus embraced human life and loved it. In the face of death, he could only place his radical trust in God, rather than in a spiritual plan of escape.

Although the Jewish people loved creation and revered the wonder of the human body, they found the prospect of God becoming human beyond comprehension and belief. They loved the created world but also respected its fragility and its transient nature. Only if we respect this infinite chasm between human flesh and the eternal word of God can we begin to grasp this stunning statement in the prologue of John's Gospel:

And the Word became flesh
and lived among us.

—Jn 1:14

The word translated as "lived among us" might be more correctly conveyed as "he pitched his tent with us." The verb (in Greek, *skenein*) literally means "to put on skin," referring to the skins from which tents were made in the ancient world. In his rather homely and playful turn of phrase, perhaps Cindy's wily little son, Jeremy, was right. In the mystery of the incarnation God has taken on "skin"—embraced our fleshly, human condition fully and generously.

13 The Immense Journey

Love is the most universal, the most tremendous, and the most mysterious of the cosmic forces.

—Pierre Teilhard de Chardin

The Incarnation Is an Unfinished Symphony

The life and ministry of Jesus represent the turning point and fullness of the holy entering into flesh. But the en-fleshment of the holy in creation is more expansive than the historical birth of Jesus. In their prayer and preaching the early communities of faith gradually came to realize that the incarnate Jesus is also the cosmic Christ. The reality of the incarnation, in other words, is multifaceted and expansive. There are many dimensions of God's nearness and presence in creation. In one sense God has been becoming incarnate from the first moment of creation and will continue to do so until the end of time. In the Phillips translation of the Hebrew Scriptures, the opening words are: "In the beginning, God communicated." This suggests that creation is itself the primal way in which God's word becomes matter, life, and flesh. Our evolving universe is the first epiphany of the sacred, the holy expression of God's inner life and mystery. Or to put it simply, creation is God's self-communication, the incarnation of the divine dream.

The awareness of creation as the "sacrament" of God has become all the more significant in the last half century of Christian spirituality. The discoveries and functional application of human science continue to revolutionize our world and our understanding of ourselves. In the stunning photographs that the Hubble telescope sends back to earth, we can actually see great star systems being born. Creation is indeed a work in progress, an unfinished symphony of God's desire to be known and heard.

Cosmologists today speak of the universe as *story* — what Loren Eiseley, in the title of one of his books, describes as the "immense journey."[16] This cosmic narrative has unfolded in four major phases or episodes:

- The galactic story
- The earth story
- The life story
- The human story

Each of these narratives shares a common source. They come from the same primal fireball of divine energy; they embody God's creative word.

What does contemporary cosmology have to do with human sexuality and relationships? As it turns out, there is a profound resonance. Dante may have been using poetic metaphor when he said that love is the force that moves the stars and the planets, but contemporary science tells us that this is more than poetry. Dante's words describe the inherent qualities of the universe. The love that continues to create stars and to shape the sprawling galaxies is the same energy revealed in the gaze of our beloved and in the affection of our friends. It is the same quiet passion that stirs in our blood and quickens our heartbeat when we are in the presence of someone we enjoy.

Evidence of the profound connection between energy and matter, between flesh and spirit comes to us from other scientific sources as well. When researchers place matter in nuclear accelerators to break it down in search of the elemental building blocks — the basic *stuff* of the universe — they discover, in practical terms, what Einstein, Heisenberg, and other physicists were trying to tell us in theory. Under these circumstances, subatomic particles exist as either particles or waves — as matter or energy. In other words, matter and energy exist in a spectrum of continuity; in a way, they are convertible. This implies that body and soul, flesh and spirit are not contraries or opposites. They are simply differing configurations of God's creative energy. Soul is not more "spiritual" than body.

The Newtonian model of the universe focused on physical things in the search for the basic building blocks of matter. The focus of contemporary science is more holistic and comprehensive. It looks for the interconnectedness of the dynamic energy fields that create such profligate and wondrous diversity. It reminds us, yet again, that the heart of reality is relationship.

When we gaze at the stars on a clear night, we are literally looking up into our womb — the birthplace of our solar system, our own tiny planet, our intricate life systems, and our own bodily selves. "Remember that you are dust," the ancient formula for Ash Wednesday reminds us, "and unto dust you shall return." Remember also, we might add today, that we are *stardust;* we are daughters and sons of the primal fireball. All of the elements in our bodies, from the hydrogen, oxygen, and carbon molecules to the more complex DNA, from the amazing sensorial maps of our skin to the intricate bio-electric systems of our brain — all of these come from the same creative source.

The ocean has almost exactly the same saline content as our mother's womb, as does the blood coursing through our veins. In our gestational life we appear to recapitulate some of the major phases in the evolution of life. In the earliest weeks, for example, the developing fetus is visibly indistinguishable from many other animal species, and at one point the developing fetus has slits like gills. "We bear the universe in our beings," writes Thomas Berry, "as the universe bears us in its being."

Cosmic Allurement

Scientists and cosmologists continue to explore the secrets of the primal burst through which the universe came into being. What explosive energy was at work in those first microseconds that is still dynamically present throughout creation — from quasars to quarks, from children at play to adults in love? Cosmologists describe three fundamental dynamics at work in this ever-expanding universe.

- *Differentiation* describes God's creative energy as it expands outwardly creating time and space. It encompasses the variety and uniqueness of every snowflake, seabird, flower, and agate, all of which reveal a diversity that is as colorful as it is incomprehensible. Each galaxy and person is unique. Apparently our God delights in such profligate variety and invites us also to rejoice in the heavens and the earth "with all their array" (Gn 2:1). The paleontologist and mystic Teilhard de Chardin refers to this phenomenon as "tangential energy" — the force that pushes forward, outward, and upward as it develops ever more organized and complex systems of physical, biological, psychic, and spiritual being.

- A second dynamic, *interiority,* implies that every aspect of creation has what Teilhard describes as "radial energy" — some "seed of consciousness," or innate capacity for interior experience.[17] Consider, for instance, the self-organizing energy of sustaining patterns and shapes around us. We notice this "within" of the universe when we gaze up into the night sky at the sweeping beauty of the Milky Way. We see it in the way Canada geese fly in formation; and we experience it in the patterns of human language, psychic archetypes, and the great stories of civilizations. Interiority drives our increasing self-awareness and self-intimacy. Without this reflective sense of "within," we would not have the freedom or intentionality to love another human person.

- The third cosmic characteristic, *communion,* is of particular interest for our reflections here. It refers to the all-encompassing reality of connection and attraction. The science of physics understands this pervasive force as the law of gravitational interaction, one of the most elemental powers in the universe. Using more theological or mythic language, contemporary cosmologists like Brian Swimme, speak of it as "cosmic allurement" or the "compassionate curve" of the universe. The Yahwist theologian/poet in Genesis and the contemporary quantum physicist share a common theme, like a recurring melodic phrase in a Beethoven concerto. Each of us carries the encoded messages of our DNA, in the cells and hormones of our bodies, in our psychic genes, and in our soul. The message reads: *"In the beginning is relationship."* Interconnection is everywhere.

14 Sexuality: The Word Enfleshed

God's language remains abstract, unreal, and ineffectual to us until it becomes embodied. But when the divine Word is embodied it communicates with life-giving power. Speech then becomes quite literally "being in touch."

—James B. Nelson

Choosing to Be En-Fleshed

In his book *Coming of Age in the Milky Way* science writer Timothy Ferris reminds us that the greatest scientific accomplishment of the twentieth century was "the discovery of ignorance" — a new respect for how much we do not know about the vast mystery that surrounds us.[18] We can say the same thing about human sexuality. Our time has plunged us into a new awareness of its beauty and its encompassing presence. Earlier we described sexuality as "energy for relationships." We can now integrate this brief description into the wider context of contemporary cosmology:

Human sexuality is the divine energy of
creativity and love,
As it is manifested in wondrously diverse forms
in the cosmos,
And as it becomes conscious and intentional
in human relationships,
For the purpose of giving life and deepening
communion.

What are the implications of this expansive vision for our personal lives? What are the consequences for our physical self-image, our affective responses, and our relationships? Most of us take our bodies for granted until we have a physical injury, become ill, or begin to feel the effects of aging. Then our physical being reminds us that we don't just *have* bodies; in some ways, we *are* our bodies. They are integral to all phases and dimensions of our lives. Discovering that we exist in an em-bodied state is one thing; embracing that condition is far more demanding. Change is inevitable, but true growth is optional and increasingly dependent upon our judgment and personal choices.

There is a difference between being incarnate and becoming intentional about the long journey toward personal wholeness. In other words, the fact that we have bodies doesn't necessarily imply that we are genuinely incarnate. Some people spend a lifetime regretting that they are embodied or looking for the escape hatch from the human condition. From early childhood they've internalized distorted religious messages or have had traumatic experiences that have produced sexual shame and guilt. Many of the people we meet in therapy have lived in conscious or unconscious repression, or its opposite — an addictive preoccupation with genital sex apart from relationships. Both repression and addiction are essentially attempts to escape the tasks of becoming truly incarnate. Incarnation is more than a condition. It is a journey, a process of befriending our flesh and then taking responsibility for channeling and directing our bodily and emotional energies in ways that are life-giving, reverential, and celebratory both of ourselves and of others.

Laying Down Our Lives in Love

An incarnational spirituality calls us to develop greater self-knowledge in our thinking, desiring, and sexual expressions. Following this responsible path demands what author Caroline Simon describes as a "disciplined heart."[19] The ultimate purpose of human life is to serve others. In Christian spirituality the model of this self-giving is, of course, Jesus himself. "No one has greater love than this," Jesus tells his followers, "to lay down one's life for one's friends" (Jn 15:13).

In recent years developmental psychology and the other behavioral sciences have also come to recognize this other-oriented perspective as a sign of human maturity. In the early years of the Human Potential Movement many of the practitioners emphasized self-actualization or self-fulfillment as the highest form of integration. But later developmental theorists, including Erik Erikson, came to realize that there is a stage of maturity beyond self-actualization, which is often referred to as "self-transcendence." The terminology may be different, but the underlying message here is essentially the same as the Gospel vision: the highest form of self-realization is a life of generous service to others.

Taking Up Our Lives with Responsibility

Jesus' teaching focuses on the necessity of self-denial and self-gift in the service of God's reign, especially on behalf of the vulnerable and marginalized. The Gospels emphasize the inner condition of the heart required to achieve this goal, as well as the role of personal responsibility and freedom in following the path of discipleship. Even as he reminds us that we must be willing to lay down our lives for others, Jesus also points to the importance of interiority, to what Pope John Paul II often refers to as "self-appropriation." Toward the end of the passage on the Good Shepherd, where Jesus lists the qualities of other-centered ministry, he also makes this significant affirmation: "The Father loves me because I lay down my life in order to take it up again. No one takes it from me; I lay down my life of my own free will" (Jn 10:18, JB).

According to the Johannine tradition, then, Jesus can be "the man for others" because he has first claimed his own authority, integrity, and selfhood. He understands others because he knows himself. He gives his life in loving service, because he himself is centered and free. In the same way, our self-giving cannot be a blind, codependent reaction that arises only out of duty, compulsion, or guilt; it must flow from a free and intentional heart. To put it simply, *we cannot lay our lives down if we haven't taken them up.*

An incarnational spirituality is about how we "take up" our lives. In practical terms, what does this mean? Let's examine three ways to take up our affective lives more responsibly.

Self-Intimacy. The possibility of authentic intimacy with another person begins with self-awareness. We all have this capacity for self-intimacy, but you have to practice it like any skill. Our identity, like all other aspects of our lives, is not a given. Moreover, there is not just one sexual "awakening" in our lives; rather there are several turning points in our psychosexual growth that call for reflection and deepening insight.

The anonymous mystic of the fourteenth-century who wrote *The Cloud of Unknowing* captures the central importance of this skill: "Should all the saints and angels of heaven join with all the members of the church on earth, both religious and lay at every degree of Christian holiness and pray for my growth in humility, I am certain it would not profit me as much nor bring me to perfection of this virtue as quickly as a little *self-knowledge*."[20]

Self-Discipline. Sexuality, as we have said, is energy for relationships. It is an intense and celebratory gift with the capacity to unify hearts and souls. But it is also a volatile and potentially dangerous force that can violate and hurt other people. Becoming sexually aroused or infatuated are instinctual and natural responses. But staying in love and directing our sexual feelings in responsible ways demand a lifetime of emotional and psychic discipline. Just as an accomplished ballerina moves with grace and freedom because she has focused her energy over years of practice, so mature human beings can enter responsible relationships when they have developed a disciplined heart and the capacity for loving sexuality.

Self-Transcendence. The goal of human wholeness and Christian holiness are ultimately the same: to love others in the same spirit of generosity that God loves us. But first we have to embrace our humanity rather than flee from it. We must also open ourselves to the journey of incarnation in the unique circumstances of our lives and come to know and reverence our sexual feelings as an integral dimension of our personhood.

In the past, certain ascetical traditions sometimes mistook denial and rejection of sexuality as the measure of true holiness, producing sincere believers with deep conflicts about the place of sexual feelings in their lives. You do not abandon your sexuality in becoming a generous, loving person. You integrate and carry this energy into the reverence and care that you have for others.

15 The Enigma of Eros

When people recognize that they are spirit in a human body and that other people are spirits, they begin to understand that our bodies are sacred and that sexuality is far more than a means of pleasure; it is a sacred act. —Sobonfu Somé

Norma Jean: Icon of the Erotic

"What does it mean that the No. 1 sex symbol of the twentieth century as voted by *Playboy* magazine committed suicide at thirty-six?" Joyce Carol Oates tries to answer this question in her novel *Blonde,* the fictionalized story of Norma Jean Baker, better known as Marilyn Monroe.[21] With her mother in a mental institution, her father unknown, and a childhood spent in an orphanage and foster homes, Norma Jean had no protectors and few psychic boundaries — only her youth, her beauty, and her sensuality to use for barter in the world of relationships. She emerged as a sex icon, but her public persona did not reflect her inner journey. In the end, Marilyn Monroe's physical beauty evoked less interest than her almost palpable craving for love, her search for a father figure, and her desire for someone who would accept and respect her as a human person. Hers is a tragic story of a quest that never met its real destiny, at least not in this life.[22]

Norma Jean Baker's life is a forceful and melancholic reminder of the power of eros in human life. In her book, Oates considers Marilyn Monroe through the prism of power and class. In the process she has also created an extended meditation on the way the erotic is experienced and understood in our culture.

What is this popular understanding of the erotic? How does it impact our attitudes toward sexuality? What does it convey about our fear of and our longing for true intimacy? What is the relationship between eros and the sacred?

The Dominant Culture's View of Eros

Our cultural images of sexuality both reflect and shape our collective psyche. Together they function as a reference point for artists and a mirror of our societal values. They can serve a vital role in our self-understanding, since they reflect the inward tension in our lives between instinctual needs and reflective desires, the spontaneous quest for pleasure and the deeper longing for communion.

On the popular level the term "erotic" carries various meanings. For some eros simply describes the realm of sex drives, the animal magnetism evoked by the rites of fantasy, seduction, and sexual liaisons. It implies those stimuli associated with sexual arousal and pleasure in the limited physical sense. In this view, the primary purpose of sex is recreation, usually without consideration for its emotional consequences or spiritual meaning.

For others eros relates more to the classic romance myth as portrayed in gothic novels or popular media. Here the drama of human passion is played out against a backdrop of personal quest, chance encounters, heroic struggles, and tragic love narratives. These stories beckon to us from the covers of *Cosmopolitan* or *Esquire* — the search for the "stranger across the room," the perfect partner that fate has destined for us. Although genuine love can come into anyone's life as an unexpected gift, for the most part, these stories are more creations of human fantasy than they are descriptions of actual relationships. Most people do not live out the film version of romance — the expectation that love will overpower us like an emotional potion, or that something magical will tell us a certain person is meant for us and we are meant for him or her.

These two understandings of the erotic — the *recreational* and the *romantic* — are probably the most prevalent images in the popular media. From billboards to film trailers, from subway advertising to the magazine racks at the checkout line in the supermarket, we are assailed with images of the physically provocative or the emotionally intriguing.

However, as in the case of Marilyn Monroe, there is a difference between the public persona and the inner life of longing. Recent studies of sexuality in America reveal that, while many individuals live self-indulgently, most people carry on fairly restrained lives. The media and advertising give us one version of the American psyche, but the majority of people are seeking — however quietly, painfully, and unsuccessfully — for ongoing mutuality and enduring love.[23] Most of us recognize that love is a demanding journey and requires responsible choices, as much as it is a pleasurable release or an exciting encounter. A commonsense realism grounds most people in the day-to-day quest for love. Most of us manage eros in the tension between private needs and spiritual tasks, between the desire for pleasure and the demands of responsible relationships.

16 Sacred Eros

The very word "erotic" comes from the Greek word eros, *the personification of love in all its aspects—born of Chaos, and personifying creative power and harmony. When I speak of the erotic, then I speak of it as an assertion of the life-force of women; of that creative energy empowered, the knowledge and use of which we are now reclaiming in our language, our history, our dancing, our loving, our work, our lives.*

—Audre Lorde

Eros as Yearning for God

Most of us feel restless in our daily lives. As creatures we are essentially unfinished, and we experience this radical openness in various ways. We know it in solitude and in community; we taste it in our salty tears and hear it in our laughter. We feel it in our weariness after an exhausting day at work or in the twilight moments before we fall asleep. Sometimes it stirs in us at the change of seasons when, in Robert Frost's image, the "last lone Aster is gone," and we watch the first snowflakes brush past our windows. We know its goodness when we hold the hand of our beloved or go for an evening walk with one of our children. We are surprised by the sudden feelings of physical and emotional intensity when we are in the presence of someone we care deeply about. We feel its tug when we say goodbye to someone we won't see again for a long time. On occasion we feel it as an almost palpable ache of the heart for a nameless presence.

Each of these experiences has something in common: they signal our yearning for human contact and ultimately for communion with God. In the end, all artistic creation, scientific discovery, philosophical insight, theological awareness, and human relationships arise from the passion for knowledge and expression. And — we believe — because our creator has placed this seeking, restless spirit within us. God is the source and destiny of this ache for wholeness. "As a deer longs for flowing streams," sings the psalmist, "so my soul longs for you, O Lord" (Ps 42:1).

Eros as Encounter with the Holy

When we seek union and communion with respect and reverence, we can have vivid encounters with the holy in the midst of life. These are times of

ARE SOME FORMS OF LOVE "HIGHER" THAN OTHERS?

In Greek, the language of the Christian Scriptures and the Septuagint version of the Hebrew writings, there are several words for love. The most familiar of these are *eros, philia,* and *agape.* Most of us would welcome a variety of words to describe something as rich and diverse in its expression as human love. But this is a mixed blessing. Although there are advantages to more precise language, we risk isolating meanings and placing a value on the various manifestations of love. This tendency to create a hierarchy of love has left much confusion and pain in its wake.

Though there are variations on the theme, depending on the century and philosophical mindset of the time, thinkers and spiritual commentators usually explain the hierarchy of love along the following lines:

- *Agape* is considered to be the highest form of love, since it embodies and reflects God's way of loving. It is generous, other-centered, and disinterested in control and possession.
- *Philia* is the love of friendship and mutuality, in which self-interest is tempered by the care and compassion we have for our family members, friends, co-workers, or neighbors.

- *Eros* gets ranked as the "lowest" form of loving, since from this viewpoint, it seeks to satisfy our physical and emotional needs instead of those of the other person.

During the twentieth century, Anders Nygren's classic work, *Agape and Eros,* revisited this familiar theme of creating a hierarchy in human loving.[24] For Nygren there is an immense gulf between eros and agape: God is the only source of true agapic love; eros is of human origin and flows from self-interest. Eros is, in Nygren's words, inherently "acquisitive and egocentric." Obviously, from this perspective, eros has nothing to do with God.

The assertion that there is no eros in God has grave consequences for how we view sexual desire and human longing. If the restlessness of our hearts and the physical desires of our bodies are not rooted in God's life and creativity, then Nygren is right — our eros has no source outside of ourselves. But this leaves us vulnerable — as the history of Christian spirituality attests — to finding our erotic selves alienated from God. Such estrangement is certainly not God's creative intention as it is expressed in Genesis and the Song of Songs. At the very least, creating a hierarchy of love seems to run counter to the affirming vision of sexuality in the Judeo-Christian tradition.

heightened awareness when we seem transported out of ourselves into a larger consciousness. There is a profound connection between such moments of contemplative experience and eros. The language for sexual union strikingly resembles that found in mysticism. The Song of Songs, as we saw earlier, can be interpreted as erotic love poetry *and* as a description of the soul's encounter with God in contemplative union. Both sexual and mystical experiences employ the intense metaphors of longing, fire, union, seeking, ecstasy, darkness and light, presence and absence, celebration and consummation. Mystics experience the underlying unity of all things as coming from one source. For Christians, of course, that source is God.

Eros as an Overflow of Abundance

Eros is not only vulnerable and seeking; it has a creative, generous side as well. When our yearning gets hints of fulfillment, it wants in turn to give life and energy to others. When we are in love, we want the whole world to know. More than just possessing our beloved, we also want to please him or her and to celebrate the abundant goodness that overflows. When our longing to create has found words in poetry or fiction, we want others to read what we have written. Long before we teach children to say "thank you," they are already expressing their gratitude by their joy and playfulness. The surest sign of our gratitude is how we praise our gifts by generating more life.

Authentic eros, therefore, is not only hungry but also creative and generous.[25] It wants to receive *and* give. Pseudo-Dionysius, the fifth-century theologian, speaks of God as having a "beautiful and good eros towards the universe." And in the same context, he describes God as creating out of an "excessive erotic goodness."[26]

17 Integrating Eros and Spirituality

The first stage is to believe that there is only one kind of love. The middle stage is to believe that there are many kinds of love and that the Greeks had a different word for each. The last stage is to believe that there is only one kind of love.
—Frederick Buechner

The Encompassing Flow of Love

While recognizing the value of making distinctions among the ways that we experience and express affection, as therapists we believe that creating hierarchies of loving helps no one. We concur with Frederick Buechner who, in the above epigraph, describes the ways in which we wrestle with the meaning of eros as an unfolding process.[27] When we are young, love is for the most part a unified experience — being affirmed, nurtured, cared for, protected, as well as learning to share and reach out to our families and classmates. As we grow up, it is natural to give greater emotional and spiritual value to some forms of love over others. But somewhere in our maturing process, we come full circle and recognize that distinctions can fracture as well as help. Beneath our grown-up tendencies toward ranking, human loving continues to flow, like a broad, deep river that carries all our relationships.

To lose oneself in another person's arms, or in another person's company, or in compassionate solidarity with all who suffer, is to find one's truest identity as a human person. In the end, these are not as much different kinds of loving as they are diverse expressions of the same sacred energy.

Learning from the Big Picture

In his important study of the relationship between sexuality and religion, Paul Ricoeur identifies three major phases in the evolution of Western understanding.[28]

Identification

In the earliest stage, eros and the sacred were undifferentiated in human consciousness. In this era of goddess worship and holy female images, sexuality merged with the people's understanding of reality through myth, ritual, and symbol. The divine presence was located, not in a transcendent world, but in the cosmos itself, especially in the generative powers of the earth and of human life.

Separation

After the emergence of the great religions, a gradual separation took place between eros and the sacred. Male gods replaced the goddess; patriarchal structure began to organize cultural and family life. Over thousands of years the sacred evolved into something transcendent and untouchable. There was a separation — at times, even a growing alienation — between body and soul, flesh and spirit, secular and sacred. Women came to embody earthy, sensuous, and procreative roles in life forces. Sexuality distracted mind and spirit and found itself limited to procreation within the institution of marriage. The discipline of mind over matter, spirit over flesh put eros into significant restraint.

Integration

Today both our religious traditions and our culture face the challenge of reuniting the sacred and the sexual in human experience. Sexuality doesn't distract from the life of mind and spirit: in fact, the sexual dimension permeates our entire being. Our sexual energy reaches to the core of our personhood and cries out for acknowledgment as a source of spiritual energy. In short, in our contemporary world we are invited to see that eros and the sacred are not enemies but friends.

How Do We Integrate Our Sexual Energy?

In some mysterious way, each of our lives reenacts Ricoeur's paradigm for the evolving relationship between eros and the sacred. It is as though each of us has the personal task of creating a *reprise* — in the musical sense of a melodic summary — of the phases and tasks of the entire human community. Our lives are like little laboratories of the history of loving, now ignited by the call to break unhealthy patterns and the invitation to journey further into sexual mystery.

When we are children all our needs intertwine. This time in our lives resembles the cultural stage of identification between eros and the sacred that we described above. Whether we are being held in our mother's arms after a painful fall or hugging a new friend on the playground, it is, for the most part, the same pervasive emotion of connection that we feel. At this stage of our development, if we are growing up in an abuse-free environment, we are literally unself-conscious. Our feelings of loving have a certain oceanic or cosmic dimension to them. Whether we are nursing at the breast, feeling the soothing warmth of bath water, comforting ourselves with genital touch, or seeing the familiar face of our parent, the sensual and the sacred converge in our sensate awareness.

At a certain point in our development, as we emerge into self-consciousness, we begin to differentiate our feelings and psychic states. We become more aware of our bodies and the emotions that surround our physical responses. In the highly sensitive area of our erotic feelings, we experience a natural curiosity about sexuality, as well as a desire for modesty, privacy, and self-intimacy. For good or for ill, we also internalize various social, religious, and cultural messages from our caretakers and surroundings. During this stage of our development — which may last a lifetime — we are aware at times of feeling strong sexual feelings and we explore and acquire patterns of behavior around these feelings, some of them healthy, others perhaps not. We come to know the difference among the loves we feel toward our parents, siblings, and friends, as compared to the intriguing, exciting, and unsettling emotions that are evoked in us when we are sexually attracted to someone or when we first fall in love.

During this time of differentiation, which is roughly analogous to Ricoeur's period of "separation," we encounter the "shadow side" of eros as well as its gifts and blessings. We come to know rejection and loss, the emotional complexity and burden, the fear and consequences of human loving. For most of us this means we pay for wisdom with the loss of our innocence. We are not speaking here about the innocence of physical virginity. Rather we are describing what Judith Viorst calls "necessary losses": the inevitable *dis*-illusionment that occurs through our attempts to explore and express — or repress — our feelings of eros, the unpleasant discovery that sometimes love *hurts*, that sexual feelings are dangerous as well as exciting, and that healthy, mutual relationships are hard work.

Most of our lives, therefore, are spent in the third task, that of pursuing integration in our sexual feelings and our spiritual values. Integration is a lifelong journey of listening to our experience with prayerful reflection. In that inward path we deepen our capacity to develop the most important human qualities of interiority, generativity, responsibility, and intimacy.

18 The Deeper Meaning of Chastity

Give me chastity and continence, but not yet.

—St. Augustine, *Confessions*

Having explored some psychological benefits of integrating the sexual and the spiritual, we want to take a bold step. We want to place this vision of psychosexual integration within a renewed and more inclusive meaning of Christian chastity. If behavioral science names the trajectory of growth toward mature loving as psychosexual development, the Christian spiritual tradition describes the same process, viewed under the light of faith, as the journey of ongoing conversion—or the practice of the virtue of chastity.

Even though there are many faces and forms of love, we believe it important to see each of them grounded in and flowing from a fundamental moral stance. This God-graced way of viewing relationships enables us to stand before other people, strangers or our most intimate lovers and friends, with a spirit of openness and reverence. Another word for this inner attitude of respect is "chastity."

Obviously this is not the usual understanding of chastity in our society. In the musical *Camelot,* Merlin sings a song entitled "The Seven Deadly Virtues." One of the lines tells us that "chastity is another word for *rigor mort!*" These comic lyrics also convey an important cultural assumption. We don't have to be social scientists to recognize that most people think chastity means prudishness, guilt, fear, or emotional sterility. For others chastity insists on a moral ideal so rigorous and beyond the reach of ordinary mortals, that it's foolish and impractical.

Reclaiming the Meaning of Chastity

In the course of Christian history, chastity gradually lost its primal Gospel meaning and became synonymous with sexual continence. While those who choose celibate chastity do indeed commit themselves to sexual continence, their way of life is defined not by what they give up, but by the relationships and generative service to which they commit their lives. Celibate chastity is far more than giving up the genital expression of sexuality. It is an alternate, freely chosen way of loving and giving life.

There continues to be widespread confusion about chastity in our contemporary culture. The average person on the street would likely not understand chastity as an inclusive virtue for all Christian vocations; he or she would simply equate it with not having sex. Likewise, in several high schools and local churches, there are "chastity programs" for youth. While many of these are worthwhile and valuable, given our culture's preoccupation with sex, this use of language has the unfortunate side effect of reducing chastity once again to sexual continence. In the long run it's not helpful to tell our sons and daughters to "just say no to sex," unless we are also helping them to understand what attitudes of respect, skills for communication, and commitment to responsible relationships they are saying "yes" to.

Chastity is the way in which the creative "yes" of love becomes embodied in our lives. In the first place, it's an attitude of the heart that manifests itself in daily life by respecting the dignity of others and following the disciplined call to integrate sexual feelings and behaviors into responsible loving. All Christians, whatever their particular vocational path, are called to live the virtue of chastity.

The word "chastity" is derived from the Latin word *castus* meaning pure, in the specific sense of being *integral* or *whole*. In Latin, one adds the prefix "in" to designate the lack of or an opposite of. Thus the lack of chastity or purity of heart is conveyed by the term *incastus*. Interestingly, this is the same word from which we get the English word "incestuous." If we understand "incestuous" in its broader meaning of being emotionally fused or unhealthily codependent, we gain insight into the word's familiar meaning. To state it in more positive terms, chastity refers to the life-long journey toward *integration*—toward being centered and free enough in our own separateness that we can enter into loving and responsible relationships with others. In the language of the Gospel, this is simply another way of saying that we cannot lay our lives down if we haven't taken them up.

In Matthew's version of the Sermon on the Mount, Jesus praises the "pure of heart," assuring them that they will see God. This original meaning of purity of heart has less to do with sexual behaviors and more with an authentic stance before God, life, and relationships. It refers to a radical willingness to practice simplicity, humility, and a spirit of utter dependence on God. It is a commitment to grow toward integration, liberation, and human maturity in the Spirit—to become whole, responsible, and free in one's relational life. This purity of heart is the basis for the word "chastity."

Reverence in Relationships

Before chastity is a moral mandate about sexual behavior, therefore, it is first of all a radical stance of the heart — a way of standing before other people. Chastity is *reverence in relationships.* It is the call to integrate eros in our lives with trust, mutuality, and respect for others. The *Catechism of the Catholic Church* describes chastity as "a school of the gift of the person."[29] If understood expansively, this is a remarkable phrase. A school is a psychic and spiritual space for the focused task of *learning.* But learning can only take place if there is a spirit of wonder, openness, and listening.

Learning requires exploration and risk; it implies that we will make mistakes and will have to return again and again to the "homework" of self-knowledge, honest communication, and a spirit of prayer. Finally, the school of chastity is one from which we never graduate. This is formation for the long haul, education for a lifetime. We never achieve the final destiny of love in this human journey, because in this school a student learns how to give the gift of oneself in reverence and mutuality to other persons.

Some Personal and Practical Implications

We have explored chastity as the "habit of the heart" that enables us to transform eros into the energy of human communion. What can we do to reach this goal? Are there some practical steps that we can take to grow in our capacity for mutuality and reverence in our relationships? The following are some initial suggestions.

Reviewing Core Life Messages

As we grow in spiritual and psychic maturity we need to become more aware of those messages — spoken or unspoken — that have shaped our fundamental outlook on life. This is especially true of the physical and emotional connections, images, memories, and values that we associate with sexuality. What were the basic attitudes and feelings about eros that you internalized from your childhood, your education, your family, your peers, the church, and the culture?

Recalling and naming these messages might involve some prayerful reflection, journaling, or perhaps conversations with a trusted family member, close friend, spiritual director, or counselor. Next, consider how these messages and attitudes have affected your life and relationships. How have these assumptions molded your experience of sexuality and your relationships? A third task involves reviewing and "editing" the core life messages around sexuality. Which of these internalized values has supported your spiritual growth? Which of them needs to be reconsidered or changed in light of deeper awareness?

The capacity for empathy is a vital ingredient in creating bonds of understanding and love. Genuine compassion involves far more than having vague feelings of caring or appearing to be a "nice" person. Our clinical and teaching experience tells us that there is a vital connection between healthy eros and an active ability to care for others. Those who are attuned to the passionate dimensions of their own lives — their affective emotions, expressive imagination, and creative interests — are more likely to effectively convey feelings of empathy and care for others. To put it simply, we cannot be *com*-passionate if we are not first *passionate.*

As an exercise in self-knowledge spend some time reflecting on what images call forth the most creative and generative energy in your life. What dimensions of your life or work most capture your imagination? What dreams or projects evoke your greatest interest and commitment? When do you feel most alive and focused? How do these "passionate interests" reflect and deepen your loving relationships? Try jotting down your thoughts or journaling. If possible, take time to share them with someone who might help you explore their implications and potential consequences in your life and relationships.

Our responses to life and people arise in different settings and are expressed in diverse ways. If chastity enables us to approach others with passionate reverence, what does this mean in relationship to our patterns of thoughts, fantasies, and sexual feelings? In a previous book (*Your Sexual Self: Pathway to Authentic Intimacy*) we described the role of sexual fantasy in healthy psychosexual development. We emphasized that sexual feelings, images, and thoughts are a natural and necessary dimension of our maturation. They help acquaint us with our desires and also set the stage for how we will approach others. Sexual fantasy is "rehearsal for relationships."

How is this so? When your feelings and thought patterns flow from actual or hoped for relationships, they help *personalize* your sexual energy, or direct your eros toward the real people with whom you seek love. For example, if you picture yourself in tender sexual encounters with a faithful and committed lover, your soul will become familiar with such a scene and come to expect it. On the other hand, if you image others as mere instruments of your gratification, you are literally "rehearsing" exploitative patterns of behavior toward others. The more you picture yourself either using others, or being used, the more such encounters will feel familiar and "normal."

Repetition of any sexual fantasy increases the possibility that it will occur in real life. For this reason, we need to make sure that the fantasies we rehearse are compatible with our personal values. Obviously, some sexual fantasies surprise us. We might enjoy them in the moment and evaluate them later. Others are more familiar — they are favorite images we store in our memory bank.

How do we evaluate our sexual fantasies? Aside from some general guidelines, putting a moral judgment on specific sexual fantasies can be difficult. Many fantasies are spontaneous, dreamlike images that are influenced by many things including brain chemistry and medication. Others arise from our earliest sexual experiences — times when sexual arousal, or awareness of our sexuality, was paired with a particular person or event. This early brain programming can be very intense and persistent:

- *When I was eleven, I broke my leg and was in traction in the hospital. A student nurse bathed me each morning. Afterwards, when the days got long and lonely, I would think about a pretty nurse taking care of me and I would feel aroused. For a long time, I felt ashamed because I continued to have this fantasy. Finally, I shared it with my wife during a Marriage Encounter. She was wonderful — she also shared some of her early fantasies with me, and it has helped me look back on this time in my life with much more compassion. I've also learned that I can change some of the imagery in the fantasy and feel more faithful and integrated.*

In general, healthy adult sexual fantasies are images where mutuality, beauty, and pleasure are present. Many people believe that fidelity and commitment need to be part of a healthy adult fantasy life — especially when the fantasy involves identifiable people or has been chosen:

- *I don't want my husband thinking of his secretary when we're making love.*

When partners are able to share their sexual fantasies with each other, a further dimension of mutuality opens up. This sharing can also help us monitor the appropriateness of our sexual images. Any sexual fantasy that involves the use of force or violence toward oneself or others ought to evoke concern and might indicate a need for counseling. The same is true for fantasies that are age inappropriate (involving minors), violating of one's commitments (a sexual encounter with another's spouse or partner), or demeaning toward anyone. Most other fantasies need to be evaluated in terms of our own personal lives, commitments, age, values, and intentions.

As a reflective exercise, take time to think about the patterns of your thoughts, images, and feelings around sexuality. Are there feelings of shame that need healing? Are there consistent narratives or images that reappear? What do they reveal to you about your inner world and attitudes? How do they reflect what the Gospels describe as "purity of heart"?

Patient Growth

None of us makes the journey toward wholeness easily. Sometimes we make poor choices that hurt ourselves and others. We might drift into self-destructive and alienating behaviors. On occasion, we overstep boundaries and violate our own standards, and in turn, we experience rejection and betrayal. Growth, especially in the area of sexuality and relationships, is difficult and demanding, to say the least. But whatever differences exist because of our vocational calling, we have the most important human and Christian tasks in common.

The deepest tasks around sexuality and relationships are those we share. This is so central that it bears repeating: whether we are married or single, young or old, divorced or remarried, male or female, gay or straight, celibate by choice or by circumstance, each of us is called to make the long and arduous journey of claiming our sexuality with reverence and integrating it with responsibility.

19 Growing Up Sexually Inside Our Faith

Be perfect, therefore,
as your heavenly father is perfect.

—Matthew 5:48

What does it mean to claim our sexuality and integrate its energies into our everyday lives and relationships? A brief look at Matthew's striking command will be helpful. Its most familiar translation is the above epigraph: "Be perfect, therefore, as your heavenly father is perfect" (Mt 5:48). We might read this and easily become discouraged. Who among us could possibly hope to achieve the perfection of God? Perfection implies flawlessness. It makes no room for limitation and does not tolerate mistakes. Perfection requires no growth. We would be complete. Is this really what God expects of us?

Matthew's context offers clarification. He is writing for Jewish Christians who would have been familiar with the Ten Commandments. Just prior to the demand to "be *perfect,*" Jesus reminds them that a literal interpretation of the laws of their ancestors is not enough. Jesus cites several commandments, one by one, and then invites his hearers to go beyond them, to do more, to keep growing: "You have heard that it was said, 'You shall love your neighbor and hate your enemy.' But I say to you, love your enemies" (Mt 5:43–44). The series of exhortations ends with the command that is usually translated, "Be perfect, therefore, as your heavenly Father is perfect" (Mt 5:48). Jesus is placing a new and more demanding understanding of the ancient laws on his followers.

A closer examination of Matthew's choice of words suggests that our English understanding of "perfection" is not identical to the word Matthew used to issue his command. You must be *teleioi,* Matthew asserts. *Teleioi* (the plural form of *teleios*) means movement toward a final end. It implies a journey toward a destiny. It presupposes that the journey is incomplete. Paul uses a form of this same word when he talks about "straining forward to what lies ahead" and "pressing on" toward the goal (Phil 3:13, 14). He acknowledges that he is not yet perfect (*teleioo*) but moving toward that goal in his life.

This understanding of "perfection" informs our journey of growth, including our movement toward psychosexual integration. It might better be understood as a command to *become whole* — to continue to strain toward the ultimate destiny summarized in the Great Commandment. We are destined to love. We are pressing toward an end that puts us in right relationship with God, with one another, and with all of creation. If we, like Paul, are straining forward and pressing on, we have not yet arrived. The journey toward that kind of wholeness takes a lifetime.

You must become whole. This message sounds somewhat more possible than the expectation that we be perfect. Since perfection is a completed state, it makes no further demands. In the real world, of course, the "state of perfection" exists only as a distant ideal, not as an actual achievement. The journey toward wholeness is far more demanding. Along its pathway we will meet discouragement and limitation. The wonderfully wild sexual energy with which God has gifted us needs to befriend our values and commitments and to become acquainted with discipline without losing its spontaneity. It won't happen all at once — we will make mistakes and know failure. We will need forgiveness and compassion, and we will need to offer it to our brothers and sisters.

20 Sexuality and Sin

I can will what is right, but I cannot do it. For I do not do the good I want, but the evil I do not want is what I do. —Romans 7:18–19

If any of us ever cut ourselves a little slack about being "perfect," it probably was not in the area of sexuality — at least not if we grew up with a Judeo-Christian background. Most of us could forgive a small failure in charity, and we generally did not lose sleep over a lapse in patience. We took a little laziness in stride, and even the most sensitive conscience could tolerate a spat with a sibling. But most of us were taught that sexual lapses were less easily forgiven. Catholics knew that the word "venial" (slight) did not apply to sexual sins. These things were more serious, even grievous, and they required sacramental absolution — the sooner the better. In the late nineteenth and early twentieth centuries, many people believed that God was somehow more offended by "impure thoughts" (i.e., anything sexual) and masturbation by thirteen-year-olds than by anything else. While this was not the actual theological position of the church, most of us got the notion that personal sexual transgressions were somehow more threatening to one's soul than other moral failures. This belief was crystallized in stories that often circulated among traveling missionaries and revival preachers:

- *Two teenagers were driving home from a dance. On the way they "made out" in the back seat (in those days this was generally understood to mean "heavy petting"). Later they were hit by a train when their car stalled on the railroad tracks, and they went straight to hell.*

No mercy. No second chance. The condemnation was as gruesome as their deaths. This story, familiar in one form or another to most Catholics and Protestants who came of age between the 1940s and the 1960s, was intended to caution teenage hearers about the "near occasions of sin," made possible though back seats and roving hands. While the intention behind stories like this may have been sincere, it helped further the impression that God loathed even limited romantic pleasures among the unmarried. Many people have told us that this negative sense of sexuality carried over into their adult relationships and has been difficult to overcome.

Conversely, some individuals have said they liked an approach to sexual formation that emphasized sin and stressed negative consequences. As one participant in a retreat said, "It did not hurt me at all to learn about the sinful side of sex. It made it easier for me to make the right choices." While this woman and others found the warnings associated with their sexuality education more enlightening than damaging, far more people who have shared their experience with us over the years hold a different view.

The stories of scrupulosity, of excessive guilt over sexual thoughts, and of a pervasive sense of sexual failure are all too common and have often had crippling effects on relationships. We hear this from Catholics, Episcopalians, Presbyterians, Methodists, as well as other persons from religious traditions that approached the subject of sexuality with a severity that was often more frightening than freeing. As one Lutheran graduate student put it, "I grew up with the message that there could be no 'slip-ups' around sexuality. No mistakes were allowed. I spent most of my adolescent years quite determined not to 'go too far.' Of course, I'm glad I didn't, but then I spent the first ten years of my marriage trying to relax enough to enjoy sex with my husband. I had developed such a rigid attitude about sexual pleasure being a 'bad thing' that I still don't fully enjoy it. There has to be a better way to communicate the values we hold around sexuality."

In their document *Human Sexuality: A Catholic Perspective for Education and Lifelong Learning,* the American Bishops in the Roman Catholic Church have initiated an attempt to find "a better way."[30] No longer dividing human psychosexual development into two stages — *before* the age of reason (when a child becomes capable of understanding the difference between "right" and "wrong") and *after* it (the rest of life) — the bishops acknowledge that persons continue the journey of psychosexual development throughout their lives. Other religious traditions have also produced a variety of fine documents that stress a developmental approach to sexuality education.[31]

Growing Beyond Sexual Sin: Psychosexual Integration

The word "integration" comes from the Latin *integer* (whole, complete), and *tangere* (to touch). Integration involves "touching in" for the purpose of bringing something to completion. It has the same source as the word "integrity." Psychosexual integration thus involves that lifelong, complex process by which we gradually come to "touch into" the depths of each aspect of our selves, joining them together into a whole. In so doing, we also move toward greater integrity and the possibility of acting out of a center that is truly interconnected.

Movement toward psychosexual integration takes us on a journey of discovery and challenge, a voyage of adventure and danger, excitement and transformation. Along the way, it invites us into a rhythm of speaking and listening so that every aspect of our identity can become acquainted with its kin: Our heads must find a way to give information to our hearts, and our hearts must learn how to get the attention of our heads. They must, quite literally, "touch into" each other. They must establish a pattern of communication as regular as a heartbeat and as spontaneous as breathing. Each new feeling must be held up to your mirror of insights, and every fresh idea must be tested in the crucible of the heart's passion. It is through this process that ideas are clarified, social interactions are evaluated, values are confirmed, feelings are understood and given appropriate expression, and passion finds its greatest enjoyment and its truest freedom.

21 The Tasks of Psychosexual Development

"What is REAL?" asked the Rabbit one day. . . .

"It doesn't happen all at once," said the Skin Horse. "You become. It takes a long time."

—*The Velveteen Rabbit*

Just like becoming REAL, growing up sexually "doesn't happen all at once." "You become," as the Skin Horse says. "It takes a long time." Few of us can document our psychosexual development in neatly progressing stages. We often encounter obstacles in our early environments that limit and sometimes even damage us. We have to do "back-up" work: recovery, relearning, and possibly psychotherapy in order to be healthier lovers and life-givers. Sometimes we cycle back again and again to heal some aspect of ourselves that has been wounded or underdeveloped. We may go through periods where we seem stuck in behavior that we can't overcome. While it may be discouraging, this pattern of breakdown and breakthrough, failing and healing, seems to be the one predictable part of psychosexual development in the human person. A Christian vision of human sexuality must make room for this uneven developmental process.

The most important dimension of psychosexual development is not how many mistakes we make along the way, but how effectively we internalize certain critical skills involved in human relatedness. What are these skills and how are they interconnected? How do they move us from the external compliance of a child to the adult who is in touch with the law written in his or her heart? They reflect the same energy that moves the planets and lights the stars.

Interiority: Deepening Awareness of Self

Like everything else in creation, we have "spirit"— an inwardness that houses a unique identity and sense of direction, guiding our role in the universe. For human persons, that inwardness is directed toward self-consciousness. Much of the journey of psychosexual development involves increasing consciousness of who we are. It includes defining our particular sense of beauty, discovering our attractions, knowing and claiming our sexual orientation, and awakening the deepest desires of our hearts. Developing a sense of interiority means making contact with the energy that will urge us to unite, to "form bonds of communion with others."[32]

As we grow in interiority, we make choices and express values that originate from within our own developing system of wisdom. Some people refer to this as "conscience," from the Latin *con* (with), and *scire* (know), literally, *to know something with oneself.* Allowing a dialogue to take place between what I have come to know and believe from within and information I have gained from sources outside myself is what is sometimes referred to as an "informed conscience." While an informed conscience is considered necessary for moral decision making, information from outside sources can never deny or negate one's own truth:

> *For people have in their hearts a law inscribed by God. . . . Their conscience is their most secret core and their sanctuary. There they are alone with God whose voice echoes in their depths.*[33]

> *It is important for every person to be sufficiently present to himself (or herself) in order to hear and follow the voice of his (or her) conscience.*[34]

The psalmist speaks of God forming "my inmost self in my mother's womb" (Ps 139:13 JB), voicing belief in a personal inwardness that exists even before physical birth. There is something "inside," some very unique identity, a sacred center that lives at the core of each person. It is here, in this most private and holy of spaces, that each of us can enter into a dialogue where, like Moses, we speak face to face with the divine.

Generativity: Growing Experience of Giving Life

As the journey of psychosexual development unfolds, we become more and more able to expand our capacity to give life. Generativity can take many forms, including creativity, work, play, invention, and, of course, biological reproduction. In the broadest sense, being a generative person means being someone who energizes others and facilitates growth. As babies and children, we develop our generative capacities by cooing and smiling, by being loving and helpful, by building sand castles at the beach and learning to ride a bicycle. Each time we delight a friend or offer a special word of encouragement to a discouraged classmate, we are learning to be life-givers. When we are good sports on a team, when we create a new recipe, when we compose a poem, we are becoming more in tune with the creative capacities uniquely our own. The ultimate goal is to become the kind of person who brings life to relationships, rather than someone who drains it.

The word "generative" is believed to go back to the prehistoric Indo-European base, *gen,* which is translated "produce." It described the task of adding to the supply of food available to the people. In the practical realm of relationships, generativity has a similar meaning. It identifies ways we "add to the supply" of resources that enable relationships to grow. It means feeding relationships, not starving them. It means behaving in ways that enhance human connection, such as having good self-knowledge (interiority), knowing and expressing feelings appropriately, being a good listener, being sensitive to the needs and concerns of others, and respecting the dignity of people. It includes the willingness and skill to face conflict when it occurs, as well as the ability to work through difficulties inevitable in human relationships.

In its more direct sexual expression, generativity refers to physical expressions of closeness, including lovemaking. The emotional and spiritual aspects of "transmitting life" ought to characterize all forms of human sharing. Whether we are hugging and kissing, holding hands, verbalizing our feelings, or having sex, there ought to be energy present that supports the relationship, helps it grow, and provides a source of fire that neither person alone could supply. Generativity does involve giving birth. It means discovering the many reservoirs of life-giving potential within, nourishing them, being patient as they grow, and enduring the hard labor of bringing them forth. When transmitting life is understood exclusively as physical procreation, the richness of human generativity is tragically reduced.

Responsibility: Maturing Exercise of Agency

Becoming responsible implies an increasing capacity to respond appropriately in interpersonal situations. The word is derived from the Latin, *respondere* (to promise in return). Growth in responsibility implies increasing one's awareness of social obligations and a corresponding capacity to honor promises made to others. Adult relationships cannot survive long or well without the mutual acceptance of responsibility for their growth.

Responsibility truly enables us to undertake obligations to another, most commonly in the form of a love relationship. The childhood tasks of bathing and dressing help teach care for our bodily selves. Being tucked in at bedtime and held when we are sick gives us the experience of being tended. Both are a necessary prerequisite to respecting and tending the body of the other. Sharing our favorite toys is childhood practice for sharing our hearts. Eating only one piece of candy, waiting for Santa Claus, and doing our homework before we go out to play help teach the discipline and restraint that are part of adult responsibility.

The young person who internalizes a sense of responsibility will become the adult who can be counted on to keep promises. He or she can be trusted to tell the truth, to be faithful, to stay with a relationship (except in cases of abuse, of course), even when things are difficult. Such adults honor commitments and are willing to do their share to facilitate the health of a relationship. They *respond* to the needs of others from within an interiorized sense of themselves and a generative desire to bring life to a relationship.

Intimacy: Increasing Capacity for Self-Disclosure

Intimacy means closeness. It involves the ability to share with another, offering the self without being imposing, and inviting the other without being intrusive. Intimacy usually implies mutuality, though sometimes one person might share intimately with another (such as with a spiritual director or counselor) when the intimate disclosure would necessarily remain one-sided.

As we pass through the journey of psychosexual integration, we become more and more comfortable with who we are, better able to express ourselves, and increasingly interested in knowing others. Fundamental to adult intimacy is storytelling, which means listening to the stories of others and learning to tell stories ourselves. Being read to, and learning to read, sharing the little secrets of childhood with a best friend, and having solitary time to wonder and be awed are all part of the early training for adult intimacy.

Straining toward the Goal

Interiority. Generativity. Responsibility. Intimacy. As we practice each of these tasks, we get better at human relationships. Studies have shown that babies in all cultures play "peek-a-boo" as part of the first stage of learning about these tasks in relationships. But none of us can remain in a baby world where we can peek out and hide again. We must emerge from our secret places and continue to risk self-disclosure. We cannot let the fleeting giggles of childhood games remain our deepest joy. The protective arms of parents cannot be exchanged for the protection afforded by masks and roles and personas if we want to experience adult forms of closeness.

But neither will we be required to leap all at once into maturity. We will need to explore the magical worlds of the curious child and love-struck teenager. We will need to have crushes and experience the sometimes wild, sometimes mundane ride of adolescent hormones, learning to experience them *and* be responsible for them. Each of us will need to discover what it means to be a sexual person. We may fall in love several times before we settle the "who shall I be with" question.

It is a long journey from "peek-a-boo" to adult readiness for an intimacy that is at once responsible yet liberating, generative yet disciplined, and ever looking outward to the needs of the other from within that sacred place of interior awareness. It takes a lifetime journey to become a confident adult who can say, "You can see me," and, "I see you," with a balanced mutuality that enables relationships to survive and even thrive. This is our destiny.

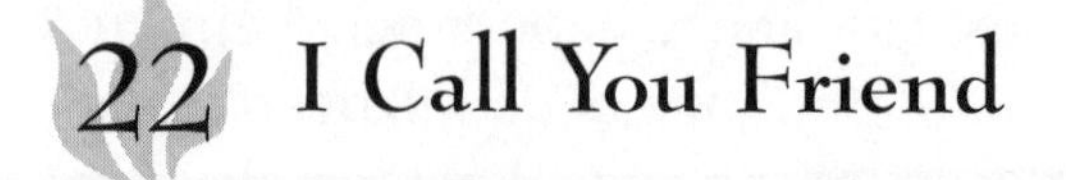

22 I Call You Friend

> *I do not call you servants any longer, because the servant does not know what the master is doing; but I have called you friends, because I have made known to you everything I have heard from my Father.* —John 15:15

Lisa and Jeff are typical of many young adults today struggling to balance their preparation for a career with their commitment to invest in the future of their relationship. After meeting and falling in love in college, they decided to wait until after graduation and getting started in their respective professions before they got married. Like most of the other couples at our marriage preparation weekend, they were serious about developing skills they would need to communicate well and deal with the inevitable conflicts that arise in relationships. But we also noticed that they were playful with each other and shared a relaxed sense of humor.

On Sunday afternoon as everyone was leaving, Jeff, who works in human resources for a large corporation, asked us jokingly if he could get continuing education credit for the weekend. “Of course,” we countered, “but on one condition — it won’t become official until you’ve been successfully married for twenty-five years!” They both laughed. Then with a look of utter seriousness in her eyes, Lisa said, “Well, that’s our dream. But if it’s going to happen, we’ll have to turn some of what we’ve learned this weekend into a lifetime of practice.”

Learning to Love

Transforming the vision of Christian loving into daily practice is not easy for any of us, no matter what our vocational path. Relationships, especially those that are close, demand a level of personal investment that stretches our imaginations and the boundaries of our generosity. Love is a crucible of human selfhood no matter what our religious perspective. But following the way of love as a serious Christian believer is particularly challenging today. The biblical vision of intimacy is in obvious tension, if not outright contradiction, with many of the images of sexuality prevalent in our culture. Is it possible to cross this chasm? How do we internalize the Gospel vision in our lives?

We cannot answer these difficult questions by repeating doctrinal formulas or giving ethical advice. Jesus tells us that it is by our *love* that others will recognize us, not by our self-righteousness. Even as we struggle against the self-absorbed attitudes of our society and the danger of being seduced by its values, we must remember our solidarity with our brothers and sisters. We may sing a different song than the dominant society, but we share the same human condition. The values we uphold around sexuality may at times give us the feeling that we are walking in exile, but these feelings invite us, not to moral disdain or ridicule, but to deeper reflection. To be countercultural does not imply that we are better than or somehow above the hopes and dreams of the more than six billion persons with whom we share this planet. The impossible dream of "living in love" (Jn 15:9–11) becomes possible only with a spirit of biblical compassion.

What's Love Got to Do with It?

Contemporary culture tends to equate intimacy with "having sex." Most of us would feel uncomfortable asking two friends who are spending time together if they have been "intimate," even though it might be obvious that they clearly trust each other, share strong values, and have excellent communication skills. We have become so focused on sexual performance that there is little room left for the more inclusive dimensions of spiritual and emotional closeness.

"What's love got to do with it?" asks Tina Turner in a popular song from the 1980s. This catchy phrase asks a vital question. Its spiritual irony implies a practical, bittersweet understanding of love and its demands. Perhaps the deeper issue is raised in another line from the same song: "Who needs a heart, if a heart can be broken?" In human relationships, the inner world of our feelings consistently reflects our lasting needs and dreams. Our hearts are the most vulnerable parts of us to be bruised and broken.

Despite the growing popularity of various remedies for sexual impotency, it is not usually the ability to perform the physical act of sex that most challenges human lovemaking. Millions of years of biological evolution and instinct have honed our response to the physical dimensions of sex. Our ability to be emotionally transparent, on the other hand, is less shaped by instinct and more dependent on personal maturity. Authentic intimacy isn't as much what we do with our bodies as it is what we do with our hearts. The demands of trust and commitment make the journey into intimacy a daunting adventure.

Most of us want to make this demanding journey, but many of us have not received the emotional and spiritual resources to do so. The challenge of integrating the physical and psychological dimensions of intimacy demands a level of maturity and commitment that eludes many couples. Despite the popular use of language, "having sex" is not always a way to experience intimacy. In many cases, the physical performance of sex is, in fact, a substitute for intimacy, or even an escape from it.

What Is "Good Sex"?

Our insistence on the emotional and spiritual dimensions of intimacy doesn't intend to diminish the goodness and celebratory nature of physical intercourse. In fact, the experience of committed, successful couples indicates that emotional and spiritual intimacy actually enhances the joy of sexual intercourse. Several studies have shown the inherent link between the ability to share spiritual values and the deepening of romantic, physical love. A spirit of vulnerability in a relationship makes it possible for a couple to take off their masks as well as their clothes. When couples let down their emotional guard, their playfulness can reveal the uniqueness of each person's inmost self.

Numerous studies have shown that romantic relationships built on the intrigue of the moment or on physical attraction alone have little chance of continuing over time. Relationships focused exclusively on sexual chemistry or infatuation are not likely to last longer than a year or two. The more genuine the intimacy in a relationship, the more likely it is to deepen and grow. No matter how attractive or lithesome our bodies might be, flesh becomes familiar even for the most skilled lovers. Without the adventure of shared dreams and struggles, without mutual commitment, most romantic relationships wax and then predictably wane. They follow what some researchers describe as the "social-exchange" theory of development. This behavioral approach to relationships focuses on the effort to maintain a balance between rewards and costs in romantic love. The personal advantages for maintaining a relationship have to outweigh the expedient reasons for dissolving it. One model of this theory is known as the "ABC(DE)'s of romantic relationships": (1) **A**ttraction, (2) **B**uilding, (3) **C**ontinuation, (4) **D**eterioration, and (5) **E**nding. Unless there is an integration of the emotional and spiritual qualities of intimacy along with the physical, the relationship will most likely not stop with "ABC," but will move through the entire acronymic sequence, from attraction to ending.[35]

What Is Intimacy?

Our Christian tradition calls us to embrace a more inclusive understanding of intimacy than what is available in the popular media. Are there certain core conditions of healthy intimacy for everyone, whether we are young or old, male or female, married, single, or divorced, gay or straight, celibate by choice or circumstance?

Like most human experiences, intimacy is difficult, if not impossible, to capture in a simple definition. Nevertheless, the behavioral sciences can help us to understand the core elements of intimacy and the important differences in expression that come from varying cultural backgrounds. From a psychological perspective, intimacy involves feelings of emotional closeness with another person and the desire to share each other's inmost thoughts and feelings. It is also characterized by attitudes of mutual trust, acceptance, and caring.

A Biblical Image

In the classroom or at workshop presentations, we attempt to ground the psychological dimensions of intimacy in the vision and practice of Jesus of Nazareth as mirrored in the Gospel traditions. In the Johannine tradition, Jesus gathers with his closest followers on the night before his death, washes their feet in humble service, and tells them, with quiet tenderness, that they are not servants, but friends. There are two different words that the author of John might have chosen to describe this friendship. The first, *hetairos,* refers to someone who is an associate or colleague. The author does not employ this word, but instead uses the term *philos,* which means "the beloved" and clearly implies deep bonds of affection.

The reason that Jesus gives for this profound level of mutuality is, in our estimation, the clearest biblical description of human intimacy. "I call you friends," Jesus reiterates, *"because I have made known everything"* (Jn 15:15, emphasis added). The key to understanding intimacy, in other words, is *self-disclosure:* the willingness to share our inner life and self with our "own." There is a danger that we might overspiritualize the "everything" of Jesus by limiting it to eternal truths or religious doctrine that he has learned from "Abba," his loving parent. In the setting in which Jesus speaks these words, his "everything" embraces the depth of his inner experience — the dreams and hopes, the struggles and pain, the poignant feelings of tenderness for those with whom he has shared the human journey.[36]

A Psychological Description

In addition to this biblical/spiritual perspective on human communion, we also propose a parallel description from the point of view of the behavioral sciences. Our "working description" in psychological terms is this: *Human intimacy is loving behavior that is manifested through self-disclosure.* This formulation has room for many circles and levels of human closeness, including persons in any walk of life, gender, age, or sexual orientation. For example, this description can characterize affective mutuality in any of the following settings:

- Spouses or lovers
- Close friends
- Co-workers or partners in ministry
- Family members, e.g., brothers, sisters, or relatives
- Parents and their adult children
- Members of a small group where there is deep sharing
- Couples who are dating or engaged
- Celibate friends

Self-Disclosure Is the Heart of Intimacy

It is worth examining this working description more closely. Most of us do not find much difficulty with the first part of this phrase, the "loving behavior." If we are attracted to someone, even if we just "like" him, we usually do not find caring actions difficult. We stay in touch with her by telephone or e-mail.

We send him a birthday card or a get-well note. If she has a cold or the flu, we make chicken soup for her. We pick up his mail if he goes on vacation. We offer to help her with projects such as mowing her lawn in the summer or shoveling her walks in the winter. We surprise him with flowers or a present on a special occasion.

For those who are reasonably mature, being thoughtful is not the difficult part of intimacy. Part two makes more demands on us: loving behavior that is *manifested through self-disclosure.* Caring actions do not reveal our unique inner feelings. And it is here — in the private world of our feelings — that we walk further into the sacred ground of intimacy. Here we also confront the reality of our vulnerability, a word that refers to our capacity to be *wounded* — to be hurt by differing perceptions, misunderstanding, or outright rejection. Self-disclosure involves the willingness to risk vulnerability in the search for deeper communion. When we begin to risk and to trust we can be sure that intimacy is deepening.

Self-disclosure isn't easy. It implies that we are first willing to engage in *self*-intimacy — the ongoing work of coming to know ourselves more honestly. "The longest journey," writes Dag Hammarsjköld, "is the journey inwards."[37] Only if we have explored the inner terrain of our brokenness and fears, our desires and feelings, will we be capable of naming and sharing them with someone we love. We cannot share a part of ourselves that we have not yet known.

The majority of communication takes place on a nonverbal level, in the "body language" of our facial expressions, the look in our eyes, our quiet presence to another person. But at some point we each have to reach inside and try to find the words for our feelings as well. Words can never adequately express our emotions, but that makes words more important, not less. Greeting card companies make millions of dollars a year on the presumption that we would rather let someone else say our words for us. But when we receive a card from someone, where do our eyes usually go first? Most of us look to see if there is a personal note. No matter how poetic or carefully chiseled the words printed on the page might be, we cherish those that are written in someone's own hand.

One of the signs of maturity is the capacity to know when and how much to disclose. It takes time to develop the level of trust and mutuality that invites another person into a deeper level of sharing. Some gifts in life, like good wine and true friendship, cannot be rushed or they can easily be bruised. The world of intimacy is not as easy or as simple as the point-and-click world of cyberspace. It doesn't help that we are surrounded by examples of inappropriate self-disclosure. We have become obsessed with personalities who reveal too much, too soon about themselves in the media or other public settings. Our fascination with talk shows and tell-all books reveals how much our society longs for human closeness, even if it is only vicarious or virtual intimacy.

23 The Many Faces of Intimacy

"But what I'm really looking for, Hugh — what I really want — companionship, Hugh — at my time of life, companionship, company, someone to talk to. Away up in Beann na Gaoithe — you've no idea how lonely it is. Companionship — correct, Hugh? Correct?"

— Jimmy, in Brian Friel's play *Translations*

The characteristics that make for holy and healthy intimacy — mutual respect, trust, self-disclosure, honesty, good communication skills, and commitment — are found in a variety of circles and levels, depending on one's job and life circumstances. While respecting that sexual intercourse is potentially the most intense and "sacramental" celebration of human love, our hope is to expand the definition of intimacy to include some of its other expressions. Here we consider three ways of understanding the everyday experiences of intimacy.[38]

Face-to-Face Intimacy

This is probably the most familiar metaphor for human closeness. It includes the many ways that we communicate directly with another person. The most obvious form of face-to-face intimacy is talk, though people in relationship who should talk don't always do so. Many helping professionals believe that "talk" is the most vital *and* missing four-letter word in the world of intimacy. In an earlier chapter we mentioned the recent study that revealed how little conversation actually takes place in most relationships, making people feel isolated and depressed.

Much has been made in recent years of the role of gender differences in human communication. A typical woman might complain to her friend: "I always have to guess at what he's feeling. He never opens up to me. It's like living next to a stone wall." Many studies have indicated that men are generally less willing to disclose their feelings, especially their more tender and vulnerable ones, perhaps in an unconscious response to having been socialized to be "strong and silent." But other studies reveal that gender differences in self-disclosure are not as great as we might presume. Overall, researchers find that women are only slightly more revealing about themselves than men are.[39] Perhaps these assumptions about gender serve more to reinforce social stereotypes than to facilitate deeper understanding. In any event, glib or over simplified approaches are not helpful to couples. Despite the popular rhetoric, men are not from Mars, and women are not from Venus. We are all earthlings, shaped from the same clay, created in the image of the same God, and sharing the same small planet. In our humanness we catch glimpses of a shared light — a light that mirrors back our heart's longings through the eyes and words of our beloved.

Side-by-Side Intimacy

In teaching or in workshop presentations, we have often asked participants what images this phrase evokes in them. We receive a wide variety of responses that reveal another, often overlooked form of human closeness. "I came to know and love my closest friend from our working together on a parish staff," a professional minister told us. "I am an introvert and it takes time for me to know my inner feelings, let alone name them and share them. But through our ministry — through the good times and the painful moments — I came to know and respect her, and yes, to love her. In the course of four years of collaborating, I discovered that she felt the same way. We now work in different geographical locations, but we stay in touch and get together to have dinner. We don't talk a lot about our relationship, but she is a true soul-mate in my life."

Other people speak about similar profiles of side-by-side intimacy. "My husband and I have the best conversations when we go for a walk together," a woman told us. "For some reason we can share more comfortably when we are at each other's side than when we are sitting across from each other at the kitchen table." "I went on a weekend camping trip with my dad," a middle-aged businessman told us. "We hiked, prepared our meals together, and sat around the campfire at night. We sipped herbal tea and looked at the stars in silence. In fact, we didn't say a whole lot the entire weekend, but I feel an immense closeness to my father now. I finally know how much he loves me."

Each of these persons describes how we can experience connection by sharing work, leisure, creative projects, or simply a comfortable emotional space with another person over time. It doesn't matter whether we call it "male bonding," "sisterhood," friendship, or emotional closeness. What matters is that it is another face of intimacy.

Back-to-Back Intimacy

At one time or another most of us have turned to a spouse, a family member, or a close friend and said something like: "Now, please back me up on this one!" Or we might have said: "I need you to stand behind me in this decision!" In doing so, we were inviting someone to enter into another dimension of intimacy. On a more superficial plane, it might have involved a colleague and the simple need to have solidarity in a project at work. At a more familiar level, we might have been asking our brother or sister or a close friend to give the support we needed to face a difficult professional or vocational crisis. In our most intimate circles, we may have been pleading with our beloved or our dearest friend to be there for us at a time of urgent transition in our relationship. Like Jesus, in his time of personal agony, we may have simply wanted someone to "stay awake" with us.

Another word for back-to-back intimacy is *faithfulness*. We all need to know that we can rely on those we love and care for. Each day we take for granted that our spouse, our beloved, our friend, or our partner is someone that we can count on. This form of intimacy is based on and reflects the covenantal faithfulness of God. In this case, faithfulness is more than a rigid, unbending attitude of life; rather it is love in the form of loyalty. In marriage and other covenantal relationships, being faithful involves the commitment to monogamy. But it also demands other forms of fidelity as well, such as the ongoing willingness to be honest, supportive, encouraging, and open to mutual growth.

Back-to-back intimacy or loyalty also has its limits. When a relationship becomes emotionally, physically, or verbally abusive, the spiritual covenant — whether in the form of a marriage contract or the mutual bond of love — is breached and broken by the perpetrator. Violence is dangerous, and true faithfulness demands that the victim choose life, even if it means leaving the relationship. Neither the Gospel nor church discipline requires an individual to sacrifice her or his integrity or personal safety in the name of a promise already broken by violence.

Love Is a Long-Distance Journey

In the end, human loving is nothing less than a search for our spiritual identity. "Marriage," writes Joseph Campbell, "is not a simple love affair, it's an *ordeal,* and the ordeal is the sacrifice of ego to a relationship in which two have become one."[40] Campbell's words describe all close relationships. The goal of intimacy is not, at the outset, to be "happy" in a self-focused or superficial sense. Rather, every mutual relationship journeys toward what Carl Jung describes as "individuation," when the mature self emerges into fuller awareness. In a deep friendship

WHAT ABOUT CELIBACY?

At a workshop on relationships, we met an engaging woman named Rebecca, who introduced herself as "an agnostic Jewish psychotherapist with a sense of humor." Early in our visit it became clear that, along with her spirit of playfulness, Rebecca was also a thoughtful and compassionate human being. At one of the more serious moments in our conversation, she said, *"I believe that a celibate lifestyle is one of the strongest political statements that a secular feminist can make in our society."*

We came away from our conversation with the deepened awareness that celibacy is not exclusively a religious or spiritual issue. Rebecca's remark highlights the diverse meanings and motivations that celibacy has in contemporary society.

In a culture in which marriage is the dominant relational paradigm, it is difficult for single persons to find a social niche or a sense of belonging in the wider community. And yet global population statistics remind us that more than half of the human community is not married. Over the years as therapists we have met many individuals who, like Rebecca, are single and/or celibate by choice or by circumstance. Some are not married or partnered because of commitment to a life project or other vocational concerns. Some are living as single persons because they have responsibilities to other family members or because they want to be economically secure before entering a committed relationship. Others have not met someone with whom they experience the level of trust and mutuality that they hold dear in human loving. Still others have physical or emotional circumstances that make finding a life partner difficult. But whatever their diversity, they share the same dreams and hopes, the same hunger in the heart for belonging and intimacy. Each of them is called to be a generative and loving person, to be a life-giver and a lover.

Finally, we easily assume that "celibate" and "single" go together. However, some couples tell us that they also experience periods of celibacy in their relationships. But this "temporary celibacy" can easily become unsettling and problematic, especially if it is not the result of mutual discussion and decision making. In the normal course of loving, a sexually expressive relationship is one of the signs of a healthy marriage or partnership. Similarly, a lack of physical lovemaking is like a silent alarm going off, pointing to a potentially serious crisis. That's why it is so important for couples to talk about their physical sharing. If, for medical reasons or other life circumstances, they choose a time of temporary celibacy, it should be a mutually agreeable decision and an invitation to deepen their relationship in other ways.

or committed relationship such as marriage, each person vows to make that journey toward maturity in relationship to and with the other person.

The journey of love is a commitment to become one's best and truest self while carrying out the unfolding tasks of intimacy. When two people — whether they are married, covenantal partners, or celibate friends — enter the dance of love, they don't do it to be "fulfilled." They do it because they're looking for their truest and most authentic selves. To hear this call and to follow it is to enter into the *agon* — the struggle of relationship. It is nothing less than an embrace of the paschal mystery.

Barbra Streisand, in her popular song "Evergreen," speaks of "love, soft as an easy chair." There may be times in relationships when love comforts as much as our favorite chair or nook. It can be a safe place that feels like home. But just as often, love is an ordeal, a harrowing call to enter a terrain that is unfamiliar and terrifying, where we enter the desert of self-knowledge and purifying encounters with the truth of our own brokenness. When Dorothy Day wrote of love, she spoke more of wastelands and vision quests than she did of romantic weekends and satin sheets. Quoting from Father Zossima in *The Brothers Karamazov,* she reminds us that "love in practice is a harsh and dreadful thing, compared to love in dreams."[41]

Both metaphors offer us versions of the truth. Perhaps, we long for intimacy that is "soft as an easy chair," so that we can embrace the times that love is encountered as "a harsh and a dreadful thing." Happiness is not the purpose of love and intimacy. But if we take on its demanding work and embrace its transforming seasons, the harvest may well be a joy our hearts cannot contain.

24 Welcome to the Table: Sexual Diversity

When you give a luncheon or a dinner, do not invite your friends or your brothers or your relatives or rich neighbors, in case they may invite you in return, and you would be repaid. But when you give a banquet, invite the poor, the crippled, the lame, and the blind. —Luke 14:12–13

Jesus tells this story at the house of one of the Pharisees where he had gone to share a meal. On the way to the Pharisee's home, he had healed a man. Since it was the Sabbath, he asked the religious leaders if one of them would rescue a child, or even an ox, that had fallen into a well on the Sabbath day. They were silent. At the dinner, Jesus notices how all the guests choose places of honor at the table, and he uses the occasion to discuss true humility. Then, in what would have seemed like a final breach of etiquette, Jesus gives advice to the host about his guest list. He tells the story of the man who gave a banquet, encountered guests who made excuses not to attend, and summoned those from the edges of the town to come to his table.

What is the meaning of this narrative in Luke's Gospel? Are we to take these stories literally, never again inviting our friends and relatives to our homes, and instead hold dinner parties for strangers?

Setting the Table in the Gospels

Meals are the most frequent setting for Gospel stories. They range from informal picnics on hillsides to banquets given by dignitaries. They introduce us to some of the most diverse and colorful of Gospel characters: a woman with long hair who washes Jesus' feet, a little boy who has loaves and fishes hidden in the folds of his robe, and a short man named Zacchaeus, who is about to have an unexpected dinner guest. Meals transport us from a wedding at Cana to a quiet dinner at a little house in Emmaus. They invite us to a party for a prodigal and let us share a Passover Supper with a carpenter's son.

Meals also function as a context for the central themes of the Gospels — abundance, forgiveness, respect, compassion, love. Here, as the centerpiece of Luke's Gospel, the dinner at the Pharisee's house brings all of these topics together in a lesson about who is welcome at our tables. This theme of

EXPRESSIONS OF RELATIONSHIP DIVERSITY

- Single adults, never married, not involved in a romantic relationship.
- Single adults, not married but involved in a romantic relationship.
- Single adults, divorced or widowed.
- Married adults in a second (or more) marriage with or without an annulment.
- Celibate priests and members of religious communities.
- Extended families living under the same roof.
- Married couples without children (whether intentionally, accidentally, temporarily, or permanently).

inclusivity is one of the benchmarks of Jesus' teaching. Everyone ought to have a place at the table, especially those who have been marginalized. Obviously, this includes many who don't qualify for the guest list — people who have been relegated to the back roads and slums of the town. When we give a luncheon, we need to make sure that no one who wants to be there is left out. Inclusivity is a

- Married people whose children have been raised and left home.
- Married priests or ministers and their families.
- Unmarried individuals living in the same dwelling either as friends or partners.

Within these examples, there is room for further variation. Individuals might be celibate or sexually active, celibate by intention or by circumstance, heterosexual, homosexual, bisexual, or transgendered. They might be disabled or physically and emotionally healthy, happy with their lifestyle or dissatisfied with it. Their circumstances might be chosen or outside of human control, such as the death of a spouse or the break-up of a relationship. In some instances, people are alone, not because they want to be, but because they haven't found someone to love.

Gospel mandate. It is not separate from Sabbath observance but a central part of it.

Radical Respect for Everyone

In Luke's time, the friends, brothers, relatives, or rich neighbors symbolize the acceptable people. They were *respected* and *included* because they belonged to the right class and practiced approved behaviors. For the most part, they would have been physically whole, Jewish males who observed the law. Anyone who did not fit this category was considered *other — undeserving of respect* and automatically excluded. The poor, the crippled, the lame, and the blind were outcast by reason of their infirmity. They represent all those who would not have had a place at the table of an observant Jew.

In this story, Jesus gives a striking example of what respect means. It does not belong to us because of our accomplishments, our personal goodness, our observance of the law, or our standing in the community. We can't earn it. What is biblical respect? It is reverence for the inherent dignity of every person as an image of God. It involves standing in awe at God's unique creation of each human being. We don't give respect only when we approve of someone's behavior, and withdraw it when we don't. Respect is not ours to give and withhold. It is the birthright of every human person.

Clearly, this story in Luke's Gospel is not about agreeing with everyone. It is not about ignoring those we love. Nor is it about careless inclusion of those whose presence would endanger others. It is about widening the circle and expanding the guest list. It is about reaching out to those whom we define as *other* — those who are waiting along the edges of the community to come to the party. It is about changing our understanding of who holds the places of honor. It is about recognizing that those regarded as *other* may have different gifts for the banquet. It is about the demands of respect and tables without hierarchical seating arrangements.

What does Luke's narrative have to do with the quest for a more liberating vision of human sexuality? How does it apply to diversity? In fact, what does the term "diversity" mean and to whom does it refer?

A Diverse Table

Diversity implies "varied." Different. The old saying that "no two snowflakes are alike" is true everywhere in our universe. No two stars are the same. The variety of species is so great we cannot assign them a definite number. Diversity is so central to the universe that without its expansive energy the cosmos would collapse in on itself. Yet contained within the mystery of diversity is the miracle of connection. Even though there are many shades of color in the universe, they can still be held together in a rainbow.

How does this apply to human persons? Is there a way to celebrate our differences and yet be held together? How much diversity can we welcome before our values get compromised or disappear? As a human community, we now have over six

DIVERSITY VS. DEVIANCE

It is important to distinguish between *diverse* and *deviant.* We use the term "diversity" to refer to the normal differences found consistently from one person to the next. In contrast, we use the term "deviance" to refer to those behaviors that violate others. For example, sexual behavior with a child is deviant. Rape is deviant. In this chapter, then, we are not addressing deviant (violating or harmful) sexual behaviors, but rather, *diversity* — differences and variations that may or may not be considered acceptable by everyone, but are not, in themselves, violating or dangerous.

billion faces. That means we have over six billion sets of dreams, over six billion stories, over six billion variations in loving and giving life. Is there a rainbow that can hold all of us? Even closer to home, can our church communities welcome all of our stories of loving? At what point does our diversity strain the quality and size of the banquet?

The Human Face of Diversity

Few people have difficulty appreciating the array of diversity in nature. Like Jesus, we notice wildflowers in the fields splashed with an amazing variety of colors and we find them beautiful. We accept without question that birds of the air live in nests and foxes choose dens as their homes. While we might disagree about the protection of rain forests, none of us is bothered by the many kinds of trees on our planet.

It is within the human community that diversity becomes troublesome. From the beginning of recorded history, human beings have not found it easy to respect those perceived as "different." The persistence of racism, classism, and sexism are evidence of our failure to honor those whose skin color, ethnic background, economic conditions, and gender are judged "less than" by those who set the table. Often, someone who is "different" creates discomfort and gets a place at the margins. This is precisely the issue that Jesus confronts. Those who are "other" belong at the table. When they are missing, something vital to our collective well-being is also missing.

Some faith communities are committed to a table large enough to welcome everyone. Others believe that there must be guidelines restricting the guest list. Significantly, the forms of diversity that occasion the most conflict usually have some connection to sexuality: Sexual orientation. Birth regulation. Divorce and remarriage. Gender equality. Cohabitation. Sex before marriage. Mandatory celibacy. Ordination requirements. Reproductive technology.

When we hear the term "sexual diversity," most of us think of sexual orientation. While this is currently one of the most volatile issues in our society and our churches, there are many other forms of sexual diversity. Some diversity is genetic, some environmental, and the source of others is simply unknown—perhaps attributable to the God who loves the sound of a soft snowfall as much as the thunder of rushing rapids, a God who couldn't imagine creating all moving water to sound the same. Human persons exhibit similar diversity when it comes to relationships. The search for love is universal, but how it is experienced and expressed varies a lot. For example, across all cultures and in both genders differences can be found in the following areas:

- Qualities that evoke our interest in, or attraction to another person.
- Ways of expressing affection, showing love, and relating to friends.
- Intensity of sex drive.
- Cues that elicit sexual arousal.
- Direction of sexual interest (toward the same- or toward opposite-gendered persons).
- Degree of connection between one's biological gender and one's gender role.

- Age-related preferences.
- Interpretation given to attractions, sexual impulses, and human longing.
- Relationship styles.
- Identification with cultural stereotypes such as masculinity and femininity.

In addition to these variations, changing customs and norms are also part of sexual diversity across the globe. One of the most significant areas of social transition today is in the make-up of the family. Sociologists report that the definition of family is undergoing dramatic change in size, composition, and meaning. Most mainline Christian denominations hold up heterosexual marriage with children as the "normal" form of family life. Faith communities of more recent origin, however, such as Unitarian Universalists, embrace all varieties of family and relationship lifestyles. While some might interpret this openness to nontraditional families as a failure to support "family values," many other believing people welcome it as a form of social evolution — a sign of humanity's collective move toward greater inclusivity, compassion, and respect.

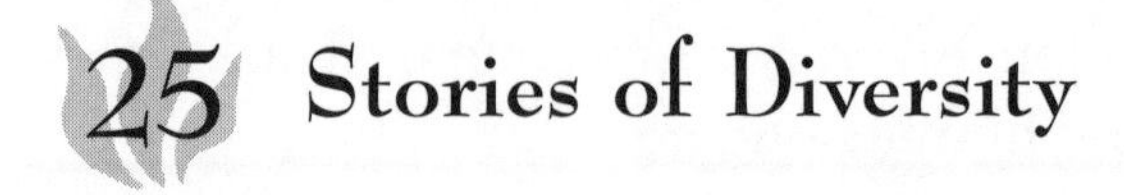

25 Stories of Diversity

Whoever receives you receives me.

—Matthew 10:40

The following descriptions do not exhaust the possible variations in sexual diversity among persons in the community, nor do they represent an attempt to evaluate lifestyles. We present them here simply because they exist. They represent real people who come to church, sing in our choirs, teach in our religious education and faith formation programs, and believe in Gospel values. Some of them "fit the norm" more than others, but all of them are struggling to find happiness and holiness in their life circumstances. Their church's current teaching may not approve of their lifestyles, a judgment that can make them feel rejected or less worthy. Their diversity falls outside of their particular religious norm. To put it simply, they are not on the guest list for the banquet:

- *When Larry and I got married, I knew in my heart it was the right thing. We love each other so much, and our relationship has been more heal-*

ing for both of us than I could ever imagine. Our children are thriving. But we had to get married outside of the Catholic Church because my annulment petition was not granted. We still go to church, and every Sunday Larry goes to Communion, but I don't. I'd feel too guilty. It's hard on all of us.

- *I'm fifty-six now, and I'm afraid to think about getting married again, at least just yet. Three failures are enough for me. My first wife was alcoholic, and my next two marriages were disastrous attempts to blunt the pain. Tina and I live together, and we've both finally found real intimacy. We're taking it a day at a time. I hope someday we'll get married, but we both have to be really sure this time. I'm a Communion minister, and Tina reads for the 10:30 mass. I guess the church would say we are "living in sin," but we have a really great pastor, and we know God understands. That's enough. I'd say we're living in love for the first time in our lives. Still, I wish the church understood people like us. We just can't make ourselves fit the category.*
- *We both come from terribly abusive families. We thought about it long and hard and prayed about it a lot. We've had our own therapy, and our relationship is strong, but we've decided to*

end the cycle. We both know we're "high risk" to pass on abusive ways, and we don't believe it would be responsible to take that risk. We're not going to have children. I got a vasectomy before we got married. We volunteer a lot at the church, and Jean sings in the choir. It's between us and God, and we're okay with it. I just wish we didn't have to feel that we were doing something wrong in the eyes of the church. They need to give folks like us more credit.

- *Lisa takes the Pill. We just can't handle any more kids and the natural family planning method didn't work for us.*
- *We are living together so we can save for a down payment on a house before our wedding next June. We can't afford two apartments with both of us in college.*
- *An annulment? No way! Our marriage failed, but it was valid. I'm not going to play that game.*
- *Bob has been gone for seven years. I'm sixty years old and I'm not looking to marry again. Tom and I have a lot in common and we enjoy each other's company. Occasionally we express our affection for each other sexually. It's not like we're teenagers. What we're doing is against our Methodist faith tradition, but we know we're not alone.*

- *Irene and I both got married young because that's just what women did in those days. She was raised Presbyterian and I was raised Episcopalian. After our divorces, we stayed good friends. Now we have grown to love each other deeply. Just because we are both women doesn't mean our love can't be real. We don't know where we fit at either of our churches, though. That part is hard.*

These are stories of real people. Most people do not make announcements about their personal life circumstances, but we know them as our sisters and brothers, nieces and nephews, neighbors and friends, sons and daughters. They watch our yards when we are away, and their children play with ours. We see some of them every Sunday in our worshiping communities. We know that their longing to feel welcome and to belong is deep and heartfelt. As one parish priest confided to us: "If everyone who didn't fit the sexual norm stopped coming to church or stayed away from Communion, we would probably have to reduce the number of services by half."

This same priest noted that many other Catholics who practice unapproved forms of birth regulation, live in irregular marriages or homosexual partnerships, have had abortions, or have made other choices around sexuality not considered acceptable no longer attend the Catholic Church. "They either recognize that their circumstances have placed them outside the norms, or they just don't feel welcome," he noted sadly. "In my conversations with ministers from other faith traditions, the stories are similar. Many people in these situations have left their mainline Protestant churches for more open communities, or simply left the church altogether."

26 Tell Us About Your Loving

Love is patient; love is kind; love is not envious or boastful or arrogant or rude. It does not insist on its own way; it is not irritable or resentful; it does not rejoice in wrongdoing, but rejoices in the truth. It bears all things, believes all things, hopes all things, endures all things.

— 1 Corinthians 13:4–7

She spoke gently, looking around the room. Her voice was barely audible at times, but her presence was a portrait of strength. "I know people are interested in scientific information about homosexuality, and I recognize that we need to know what our religious traditions teach about it. But sometimes, when sexual orientation is discussed, I wish I could feel less like a laboratory subject and more like a regular person. I keep hoping people will stop asking, 'What causes homosexuality?' and instead say, 'Please tell us about your loving.' Then this would feel more like a Christian community that respects me instead of one that wants to analyze me."

A graduate student preparing for ordination in the

United Church of Christ, Kathleen was only twenty-four. Already, negotiating the world as a young lesbian woman was a daily challenge for her. She choked back tears as she told us how it felt to hear the comments of other students who had been engaged in an earlier discussion about the causes of homosexuality. "I don't think anyone really knows for sure," one of her classmates had said, "but I've heard it's at least partly genetic." "It probably gets determined before birth," added another. "Well, whatever," chimed in a third with a tone of practical detachment, "we still need to do something to help them feel welcome in our faith communities without directly advocating a homosexual lifestyle."

Should Anyone Be Invisible at the Table?

As conversations on the subject of sexual orientation go, this one sounded fairly innocuous, perhaps even supportive. But for Kathleen, it was one more discussion that left her feeling like the invisible *other* — someone whose love energy was put out for debate while she silently listened and agonized from the sidelines. Her sexual orientation was a condition to study, a problem to solve, or, on some of the worst days, a joke to laugh at over lunch. Even though she was studying in a seminary known for its openness and its strong stance toward justice, Kathleen had to steel herself daily for the possibility of humiliation. "I think the hardest part," she confided, "is that my way of loving is talked about as an entity in itself, as though it has no necessary connection to me, or to any real life gay or lesbian persons who laugh and cry, feel affection, fall in love, and try to make a relationship work. It is as though our collective hormones and genes are more important than our thousands of stories of loving."

Respect and Sexual Orientation

Most faith traditions mandate respect for the human person, but not all would interpret this to mean acceptance of same-gender relationships. It might include respecting homosexual persons, while rejecting what is sometimes called a "homosexual lifestyle." Sexual diversity, in the minds of many, is a misnomer. "God created us male and female and told us to go forth and multiply. That's just how it works. I don't understand all this talk about sexual diversity when it means two members of the same-gender having sex." This statement, expressed by a young Presbyterian mother, gives voice to the official position held by most mainline religious groups. It does not make room for Kathleen, or any of her gay and lesbian brothers and sisters.

Did God create human persons to fall in love outside the confines of heterosexuality? This is the conviction among those who believe that same-gender love expresses acceptable sexual diversity. "Love is what is important. It is the heart of the Christian vocation. God created the universe with diversity in all other areas. It is difficult to believe that such a God could imagine only one acceptable way in which human love could be expressed sexually. Same-gender love might even represent a natural way of limiting overpopulation." This statement, spoken passionately by an Episcopalian minister whose son is gay, resonates with many in our church communities who find no contradiction between fidelity to Gospel values and faithful, committed love between two persons of the same gender. Studies suggest that this group is gradually becoming the majority of mainline believers.

"Our churches need to continually challenge us to be loving people. Sometimes we get sidetracked by the rules we've made and lose sight of the big picture." The woman who spoke these words was convinced that most denominations are overly preoccupied about sex outside of marriage between single adults who love each other—whether the relationship is same- or opposite-gendered. "I would like to hear all of our religious institutions speak more forcefully against the sexual behaviors that truly represent a *danger* to the family and community," she added. "What is more dangerous for children? Being around a gay or lesbian couple who love each other or around a heterosexual couple engaged in domestic violence?"

These young Catholic mothers at a retreat were expressing a belief we as therapists have heard articulated repeatedly — that Christian communities ought to be known for their compassion, love, and respect. Actions that destroy or violate relationships should be the primary concern of the community. Thoughtful, committed Christians are reconsidering the conditions that contribute to a wholesome family environment. They are reimaging the requirements for holy and healthy expressions of love between adults. Increasingly, *belonging* and *being seen* in our communities are rights that ought not be forfeited by anyone who takes seriously the call to love.

27 Struggling with Guidelines for Belonging

It is only with the heart that one can see rightly; what is essential is invisible to the eye.

—Antoine de Saint-Exupéry

Why is this issue of lifestyle diversity such a difficult one? The answer is related to the nature and meaning of *belonging*. Virtually all organizations have guidelines for membership. In general, if we keep the rules we can stay, if we break them we're out. We recognize this from the early clubs we formed as children, often posting our handwritten mandates on playhouse doors and tree trunks with rickety steps leading to a fortress in the branches above. We know it from Scouting, from 4-H, and from fraternity and sorority houses. We can find membership regulations for most of the organizations to which we belong as adults. Even our credit card companies take away our plastic if we don't honor their requirements. With very few exceptions, most religious institutions also provide guidelines for membership. Unitarian Universalists have the fewest guidelines — they have no particular creed, inviting people to formulate their own personal credos. A member of this church recently shared with us the difficulties that this degree of openness can pose in a congregation:

> *One of our foundational principles is that everyone respect the dignity and beliefs of everyone else. Recently, we had a family join the church whose two teenaged sons were skinheads. This posed a problem, since it seemed to fly in the face of our commitment to respect everyone. When these boys began wearing T-shirts with racist slogans to church, we confronted them. They told us that they had a right to have their beliefs respected, just like everyone else in the congregation. We sometimes experience the limits of the kind of openness that we're committed to. Many church members are raising the issue of clarifying membership guidelines.*

Most people agree that organizations need to have some criteria for belonging. There is a difference between "opening wide the doors to Christ" — the millennial theme in Roman Catholicism — and taking the doors off altogether. But what should these criteria be? Who decides what they are? Do they all have the same weight, or are some more essential than others? And at what point ought our

THE ISSUE OF BELONGING IN EARLY CHRISTIANITY

The issues around diversity and belonging are not new. They have been with us since Christianity's earliest days in Jerusalem. The tensions were described in language and categories different from ours, but they were no less urgent or divisive. Can Gentiles be allowed into the community? What about the uncircumcised? Are we to relax our rules around ritual purity or impose them on everyone who wants to be part of us? Even Peter and Paul did not agree on these issues.

The Acts of the Apostles gives an account of Peter's dramatic movement toward inclusivity and the challenge it posed to the community of believers at the time. While he was at prayer, Peter's categories of acceptability are shattered by a voice from heaven saying, *"What God has made clean, you have no right to call profane"* (Acts 11:10). Peter interprets this message as a challenge to the Jewish law forbidding the Jews from mixing with and visiting people of a different race. Immediately following this experience, Peter is summoned by the Spirit to go to the Gentile household of Cornelius and preach to the people assembled there. After the gift of the Holy Spirit is poured out on them, Peter orders all of them to be baptized. But his community at home was not pleased. When the circumcised apostles in Judea heard of this, they confronted him saying, *"So you have been visiting the uncircumcised and eating with them!"* (Acts 11:3–4). Peter defended his actions with a detailed account of his experience, ending with a description of the Holy Spirit coming down on the Gentiles *"in the same way as it came on us at the beginning . . . and who was I to stand in God's way"* (Acts 11:15–17). This satisfied the apostles from Judea. But, as Christian history attests, the issue of belonging is far from resolved.

If the Christian communities closest to the words and memory of Jesus had problems agreeing about membership requirements, it should not surprise us that we have difficulty with this as well. In the end, we can follow their example only by carrying the struggle forward and by responding to each new situation with as much conviction and openness as we can. Like the apostles in Judea, we can raise our concerns. We can challenge and confront one another. And like Peter, we can tell the story of our experience. And then get out of God's way.

failure to honor the criteria for belonging result in our being excluded from the table? These are difficult questions, especially when they come to issues surrounding sexuality and relationships.

We all fail to live up to the demands of Gospel living, yet our failures in charity, our impatience, and our judgmental attitudes do not get us excluded from our worshiping communities. Many of us don't live in accord with our particular church's teachings in many areas, social justice being one of them. Many members of mainstream Christian religions even regard social justice as unessential to the practice of one's faith. This is not cause for us to refrain from singing in the choir, sitting in the front pew at a worship service, or receiving Communion.

The leadership of the Catholic Church often shows great tolerance for those openly opposed to the more progressive teachings of the Second Vatican Council, commonly making special concessions for them. Suggesting that they refrain from receiving Communion until they conform to the teachings of the Council would be unthinkable. What is it about the issues around sexuality, lifestyle, and relationships that are different? Why is it that kind, generous, loving, divorced Catholics, who have remarried without an annulment, are no longer welcome at the Eucharistic table unless their relationship is celibate? Why is a Presbyterian gay man, living in a committed and faithful partnership for fifteen years, excluded from ordination in his faith community? These situations seem to make *genitality* rather than *love* the defining test for Christian authenticity — something difficult to reconcile with the preaching and teaching of Jesus.

28 Roman Catholics, Sex, and the Eucharist

This is my body which is given for you. Do this in remembrance of me. —Luke 22:19

The Eucharist is *the* banquet, the sacramental sign of the heavenly feast for Roman Catholics. Receiving Communion is the ultimate ritual of belonging. Divorced persons who have remarried without annulments are welcome to attend the liturgy and other parish functions. So are people of other faith traditions, relationship status, or sexual circumstances. Receiving Communion, however, is restricted to those whose participation gives witness to the Eucharist as the sacramental sign of the reign of God to come.

While some find reassurance in this, others find it troubling. For this latter group, inviting people to a community celebration, and then excluding some of them from the meal, is not a sign of the heavenly banquet. In a recent discussion, one of our students expressed it in these words: "I cannot imagine inviting all of my relatives over to my home for Thanksgiving, including everyone in the sharing of stories and visiting, and then, just as we are about to eat, discreetly ask my Uncle Harry and Aunt Martha to remain in the living room because their irregular marriage doesn't meet with our approval." While this student was quite animated about her feelings, others were equally intense on the other side, insisting that the Eucharist would have no meaning if anyone could receive it.

What is the key to understanding these differing viewpoints? Why do some people approach the Eucharist as a sign of acceptability and shared orthodoxy, while others view it an opportunity for welcome and inclusion? The answer lies in two differing ways of understanding the nature and meaning of the Eucharist, both of which have roots in our biblical and spiritual tradition.

Eucharist: Sign of Union Already Achieved

The first of these perspectives is the current official practice in the Roman Catholic Church. It understands the Eucharist as a *sign of unity already achieved.* Those who come to the table do so precisely because they are already "in communion" with the teaching church. Their participation in receiving the bread and wine, the Body and Blood of Christ, signals their current unity with all the other believing members of the community — a unity manifested by a lifestyle in keeping with the practice of the Catholic faith. According to this view, the meaning of Eucharistic participation would be endangered if those who came to the table were not living in accord with the teaching church. This understanding of the Eucharist is also associated with the need to be in the "state of grace" before receiving Communion — hence the practice (less common today) of receiving the sacrament of reconciliation ("confession") prior to going to Communion.

Eucharist: Food for the Journey Not Yet Completed

There is another understanding of the Eucharist that also has ancient roots in our tradition. In this view, the Eucharist is a *source of forgiveness, healing, and reconciliation.* It is *grace* — that is, freely offered nourishment for the journey, a communal sign of God's unconditional love. Those who come to the table recognize that they are sinners longing for healing. They come not because they have *achieved* communion but because they *need* it. They are seekers yearning to be fed by the sacramental presence of the risen Christ. In this approach, we come to the table, bringing our woundedness, our inability to live up to the demands of the Great Commandment. We also come bringing our hunger, our resilience, our hope, and our gifts, however limited they might be. When we arrive at the table, we meet others like ourselves: the blind and the lame, the poor and the crippled. We encounter a little boy sharing loaves and fishes and a woman anointing feet. At this table we recognize that we are all in some way "outcast" and, at the same time, gifted. Sometimes we may come feeling more gifted and generous. At other times we may feel more broken and needy. But always, we are welcome.

As Christians, we believe that we are "one in Christ," that there are "no distinctions" based on our differences. Though much remains to be done, we are making slow progress in confronting racism, classism, and sexism in most of our church communities. We are trying to create inclusive communities where *belonging* is not conditioned by skin color or gender, by economic privilege or lack of it, by age, disability, or political viewpoint. But the issues surrounding sexuality and relationships continue to be difficult and persistent challenges. They call us to reexamine our understanding of respect and inclusivity, as well as our motivation for excluding certain groups of people.

Eucharist as Both Sign and *Source of Human Communion*

To what extent can the Eucharist be *both* a sign of a communion already achieved *and* a source that brings about unity? Can our churches hold up the value of marriage *and* at the same time welcome those who do not fit the official norms? Can we continue to affirm our belief in permanent commitments *and* at the same time create a welcoming space for divorced persons? Can we offer opportunities for healing after divorce without necessarily burdening people with the complex and sometimes humiliating process of annulments? Can we believe in traditional family life, *and* also set a table where people in other experiences of family will find a place card with their name on it?

The challenge before us is a daunting one. It involves our ability to hold the values of the Gospel in a creative tension. In practice, this means that we must find a way to honor both our ethical vision and our summons to compassion, our call to moral responsibility and the demands of inclusivity. Our ability to balance these values may well "make us or break us" as a community of believers. Why? Whenever the teaching and practice of a religious institution become separated from the lived experience of its people, or whenever that institution is more focused on maintaining the status quo than preaching the Gospel, it is in danger of losing its credibility and its sense of mission. People will no longer look for guidance from a religious institution too far removed from their own convictions and practice. They will not maintain membership in a church that appears to have lost connection with the real-life values, needs, and beliefs of its people.

29 Toward a Spirituality of Relationships

By this everyone will know that you are my disciples, if you have love for one another.

—John 13:35

Jesus had a wide list of possibilities to choose from in deciding what would be the identifying sign of discipleship. Given his Jewish prophetic roots, he could have named justice as the benchmark of a faithful life. As part of the rabbinic tradition, he might have chosen keeping the Torah as the ultimate ethical test. As a member of the priestly people of Israel, he could have held up worship and sacred ritual as the cornerstone of religious observance. He might have selected any of these or some other quality of life to characterize his followers. But Jesus chose *love.* "By this everyone will know that you are my disciples — if you have *love* for one another." More than any other attitude or behavior, loving is the mark of a Christian.

But what attitudes and actions are included in Jesus' mandate? What do we mean by love? In the past, some believers have understood this command to love as limited to those acts of service and self-sacrifice reflected in the life of Jesus, especially as they culminate in his suffering and death. Certainly, there is good reason for seeing this as the premier expression of love. In the Synoptic tradition words similar to those in the above epigraph would have been spoken at the table of remembrance, where Jesus gave us the Passover bread and wine as the sacrament of his broken body and his blood poured out for all humankind. In John's Gospel, these words occur just after Jesus has taken off his garments and washed his disciples' feet in the role of a servant. For Jesus, love and service, even unto death, are inextricably linked.

We believe, however, that Jesus' words cannot be limited to any specific act or gesture. He is speaking less about the outward appearance of compassion and more about the inner eye of love. He is calling us to a fundamental attitude—a stance of the heart—that must motivate all loving, whatever its pattern or expression. Whether it is a single parent caring for a sick child in the middle of the night, a husband and wife holding each other in intimate physical union, or celibate friends sharing a warm embrace, all of these expressions of love flow from and find their model in the *caritas* of Christ. Love has many faces, eyes, hands, and expressions, but it has only one heart. "God is love," the first letter of John reminds us, "and those who abide in love abide in God, and God abides in them."

Intimacy is a way of describing the manner in which love is embodied and manifested in our closest relationships. It encompasses the mysterious terrain of mutuality as it is expressed in the affective, reverential, and tender forms of communication and sharing in our lives. "Sexuality affects all aspects of the human person in the unity of body and soul," the *Catechism of the Catholic Church* tells us. "It especially concerns affectivity, the capacity to love and to procreate, and in a more general way *the aptitude for forming bonds of communion with others.*"[42] In our communities of faith and in our society, there is a renewed urgency to develop a more inclusive spirituality of relationships. Unlike the dominant culture, we refuse to limit intimacy solely to its physical expression in sexual intercourse. And unlike some spiritual commentators, we see all forms of intimacy, including the romantic and physical, as potentially whole and holy manifestations of the command to love. If love is a rainbow, intimacy is one of its primary colors.

On the night before he died, John's Gospel portrays Jesus as gathering "his own" for a meal of farewell. During the supper, Jesus shares his final hopes and vision with his followers in what we have come to know as "the last discourse." In these final reflections, Jesus prays for unity among his followers and ultimately among all human persons: "May they all be one. As you, Father, are in me and I am in you, may they also be one in us, so that the world may believe that you have sent me. The glory that you have given me I have given them so that they may be one, as we are one" (Jn 17:21–22).

In these words the contemporary church sees an archetypal image for human intimacy as rooted in God's own inner life. In this passage Jesus "has opened up new horizons closed to human reason by indicating that there is a certain similarity between the union existing among the divine persons and the union of God's sons and daughters in truth and love."[43] Studies in cross-cultural anthropology and in the behavioral sciences have given us an expansive understanding of the beauty and diversity of human intimacy. But, as helpful and necessary as these human disciplines are, they cannot provide us with the meaning that comes from seeing human love as rooted in God's inner life of communion. We come to know the breadth and length, the height and depth of love, the mystery that "surpasses all understanding" (Eph 3:18–19), only through the eyes of faith.

When we listen to and respond to the stirrings within us to love and be loved by another human person, we are following a primal instinct. When we take the risk of authentic intimacy, we embark upon an adventure in friendship or romance. When we say with our words and with our behaviors, "I love you," we become more human. But in becoming more human we also participate in a deeper mystery. When we choose to love, we activate the image of God in us. When we enter the world of intimacy, we are literally embodying the Great Commandment. We are making God's inner life of union and communion more visible and present in this life.

Love as Intimate Knowing

From the sacred stories of our Judeo-Christian tradition we inherit a rich set of images surrounding human intimacy. In the Hebrew language, one of the words for intimacy is *jadac*, "to know." For many of us in contemporary Western culture, this is a puzzling use of language. We tend to associate knowledge with philosophical theory, scientific hypotheses, or—in today's cybernetic world—with extrapolation from data. While it can also have the connotation of intellectual comprehension, *jadac* usually refers to concrete, personal knowledge, such as the experience of suffering (Is 53:3), of sin (Wis 3:13), of war and peace (Is 59:8). It also applies to the experiential process of confronting our moral choices through the "knowledge of good and evil" (Gn 2:9–17).

This is also the word that is used to describe God's profound "knowing" of our inmost self and our behaviors (Ps 139), as well as our experiential knowledge of God (Jer 31:34, Jn 14:9). The Fourth Gospel explicitly links this kind of intimate knowledge to our destiny as pilgrims and disciples: "This is eternal life: to know you the only true God, and Jesus Christ whom you have sent" (Jn 17:3). For Jesus, loving God is equivalent to "knowing" God, i.e., coming into an intimate relationship with one's whole being and life commitments.

One of the most striking uses of *jadac* in the Pentateuch is to convey the meaning of sexual intercourse: "Now the man *knew* his wife, Eve, and she conceived and bore Cain" (Gn 4:1). This use of the term "to know" is laden with a rich connotation that invites us, in the first place, to deepen our perspective on the spiritual meaning of sexual intercourse; and, secondly, to expand the meaning of intimacy to nongenital forms of communion. In his theological and pastoral reflections on this passage, Pope John Paul II makes an insightful observation: "We can see in this [use of the term *jadac*] a sign of the poverty of the archaic language, which lacked varied expressions to define differentiated facts. Nevertheless, *it is significant that the situation in which husband and wife unite so closely as to become one flesh has been defined as knowledge.* In this way, from the very poverty of the language a specific depth of meaning seems to emerge."[44] And perhaps, we might add, that the seeming "poverty" of language in this instance carries a quiet invitation to be more spiritually inclusive when we speak of human intimacy in its many expressions.

30 The Biblical Vision of Loving

Jesus loved Martha and her sister and Lazarus.

—John 11:5

If we could set aside our cultural and religious preconceptions and read the Bible as literature, we would likely be surprised at both the earthiness and realism with which our spiritual ancestors approached human intimacy. Unlike the surrounding cultures, the Israelite people "demystified" sexuality. They did not worship it, but viewed it as a precious and challenging dimension of being a creature. They also had an instinctive appreciation of its ambivalence, with the result that they report its many expressions — the tender, the brutal, and the erotic — with a matter-of-fact attitude that might shock the unsuspecting pious reader. Whether we are reading about Noah's drunken near-incest with his daughters, Rachel's barrenness, Jacob's dysfunctional family, David's wandering eye, or Qoheleth's sexual malaise, the struggling human condition is acknowledged and given a wide berth. One almost gets the impression that sexuality and intimacy are approached with an attitude of bemused realism. As one Jewish writer aptly puts it, "How like a people who have God in the head to insist that God is in their loins too!"[45]

In this context of spiritual realism we can better appreciate the more inspiring portraits of intimacy in the Hebrew writings. Their diverse images of tenderness, erotic passion, mutuality, and undying friendship often defy the social and religious conventions of the time. If we remember, for instance, that mutual, loving intimacy was not presumed or even expected in the Jewish marriages of the time, then the Song of Songs might well be understood — along with several other interpretations — as a countercultural celebration of mutual intimacy and passion in relationships. Similarly, Ruth and Naomi forged their bond of faithful friendship and loving sisterhood in a man's world, where unattached women had little or no social identity and even less psychic and physical safety. David and Jonathan risked their social standing and their very lives to leave us a larger-than-life profile of male friendship.

But these are not just moving stories of human love and friendship. In the Israelite spiritual tradition they must be understood in light of the *covenant.*

God's love for the chosen people is the model for every human relationship. Thus, the reciprocal love between the Shulamite and her beloved shepherd, the undying faithfulness between Ruth and Naomi, and the enduring friendship of David and Jonathan find their ground in God's way of loving. Each of them is a reflection of God's *hesed rahamim* — the "womb-love" of God expressed in faithfulness and ongoing compassion. This form of intimacy transcends the boundaries of birthplace or ethnic heritage or the conventions of romance, because it flows from God's own desire for intimacy.

Mutuality and Respect

Despite the varying theological concerns of the individual evangelists, a composite human portrait of Jesus emerges. Beneath the miracles and ministry of healing, behind the parables and discourses, we see the outline of a person who lived his life with passion and cared for people with a fierce tenderness. From the beginning, Jesus lived a *relational* life; he chose not to "go it alone." This does not mean that he avoided solitude or that he never felt abandoned. Jesus faced the loneliness of carrying his life and his vocational path. He knew that his ministry would place him at odds with the religious and political institutions of his day. Given this reality, it is understandable that he frequently sought out times of solitude and prayer. But he never chose a pathway of isolation. He was not a "spiritual lone ranger," who appeared on the horizon of history, saved humankind from its brokenness and sin, and then disappeared into a celestial sunset.

Before Jesus healed a leper or cast out a demon, before he told a parable or multiplied loaves, he began to form a community of women and men around him. It is a simple fact that we dare not take for granted: the one whom Christianity claims as Lord and brother, chose not to be a "solo savior." Instead he entered into the mystery and the pain of human relationships.

In Jesus' life, as in ours, there are many circles of relationships and levels of intimacy:

- *The crowds.* In the widest circle there were the crowds that came and went in his life, some of them suspicious and inimical, many of them desperate for healing and wholeness, most of them merely curious or hoping to see wonders. This is hardly a portrait of what we would ordinarily describe as intimacy, and yet, the Gospels remind us repeatedly that at the sight of the crowds, Jesus was moved with compassion. He reached out to welcome them, to heal and console them, "because they were harassed and helpless, like sheep without a shepherd" (Mt 9:36).

- *The seventy-two.* The next circle of relationship is portrayed in the seventy-two disciples that Jesus sent forth in his name. Who were these ministry partners, and what was their relationship with Jesus? Some scholars believe that this group may embody a biblical image of mutuality and solidarity that reflects the earliest post-Resurrection movements of evangelization. Some of them would have been married couples, others celibate. The two disciples on the road to Emmaus reflect this partnership ministry and its spirit of intimacy with Jesus. It is a story of encounter and dialogue along the way, a narrative about deepening trust and relationships. The words and images speak to us of intimate and passionate communion: the partners asking Jesus to stay with them, their coming to "know" him in the breaking of the bread, and the haunting memory of their hearts *burning* within them (see Lk 24:13–35).

- *The Twelve.* Each of the Gospels gives us a version of the personal call of the Twelve who would become the new sons of Israel — the founding partners of the new people of God. Here we see reflected a deepening spirit of intentionality and mutuality on Jesus' part. In the striking words of Mark, Jesus "went up the mountain and called to him those whom he *wanted,* and they came to him. And he appointed twelve, whom he also named apostles, *to be with him,* and to be sent out to proclaim the message" (Mk 3:13–14, emphasis added). For Jesus, ministry is not just a religious function; it is grounded in relationships and community.

- *The Three.* Within the circle of the twelve, Peter, James, and John appear to have enjoyed a particular closeness to Jesus. They accompany him and share his transforming experience on Mt. Tabor. They are constantly at his side during his ministry of healing and preaching. They remain close to him when he withdraws into deserted places for prayer and rest. Jesus, in turn, pleads with them to stay awake with him during his hour of need in the garden of Gethsemani. Even given the bickering about power and position among the Twelve, it seems assumed that Jesus will choose some who are his closer associates.

- *The Inner Circle.* As God's servant, Jesus called together various circles and levels of disciples and fellow ministers. But the Gospel profile also speaks of relationships that Jesus had which, to all intents and purposes, went beyond ministry to the human need and gift of friendship. These persons are, in the truest sense, the "inner circle" of Jesus' life. The Gospel of John acknowledges this simply: "Jesus *loved* Martha and her sister and Lazarus" (Jn 11:5, emphasis added). The history of Christian spirituality reveals a certain embarrassment with the prospect that Jesus might have strong affective feelings for other people. As a result, we have tended to reduce the love that is described here to a generalized compassion or, at the most, a warm attitude of caring. Perhaps this says more about our uneasiness with human intimacy, than it does about Jesus' actual feelings and needs.

Was Jesus Sexual?

If sexuality is a God-given energy that draws all of us into relationships of love and care, then Jesus is among the most sexual beings who ever lived. The story of his life is filled with intimate encounters with other people, and he made loving the primary mark of discipleship.

But did Jesus' sexuality include genital expression? Tradition asserts that he was unmarried and therefore celibate throughout his life. A similar assumption might have been made about Peter and the other apostles had we not been told that Jesus healed Peter's mother-in-law (Lk 4:38). In the patriarchal world of Jesus' day, women were rarely mentioned unless their stories served to highlight some significant event or truth. Did Jesus have a wife whose existence and identity never needed mentioning? Or was Jesus one of the itinerant preachers, common in biblical times, who remained unmarried because of the urgency of his mission? While biblical scholars continue to explore this subject, we can be certain about a few things:

- The Scriptures are silent about Jesus' marital status.
- Jesus *"increased in wisdom and in stature"* (Lk 2:52). Normal human growth includes psychosexual development, with its attendant physical and hormonal changes, sexual arousals, and, in the case of males, spontaneous erections and ejaculations. Jesus was not exempt from normal human development. (An early heresy, or false teaching, called Docetism proclaimed that Jesus only *seemed* to have a human body).
- Jesus was fully human, *"one who in every respect has been tempted as we are, yet without sin"* (Heb. 4:15). Anyone who is fully human experiences emotions, feelings, and attractions. Since sexual feelings are not sinful, but rather are

part of God's good creation, we can assume that Jesus experienced them.

The biblical evidence leaves us with more questions than answers about the personal ways Jesus experienced his sexual energy. And yet, we instinctively know that only a person acquainted with *eros* could speak with such tenderness and love toward those with him at the Last Supper (Jn 13:33–17:26). We can assume that only someone comfortable with human touch would welcome a woman washing his feet with her tears, kissing and caressing them with her hair in one of the most sensuous stories in the Scriptures (Lk 7:38). Even our uncertainties about the specifics of Jesus' personal life invite us to look closer at what is significant. His speaking, touching, healing, weeping and leaving give us a portrait of sexual energy in all its rich diversity, complexity, and passion.

If someday we were to learn that Jesus was married, that he made love with the same sensitivity, intensity, and passion that energized his ministry, would it make a difference for our faith? If such a discovery would trouble us, perhaps this says more about our attitudes toward sexuality than it does about Jesus. In the end, his marital status is not the real question. Was he faithful to his commitments? Did he love with whole-hearted passion?

HOW SHOULD WE LOVE?

In our work, we often hear students, young couples, and others ask a variety of questions about sexuality that, taken together, echo the familiar: *"How far can we go?"* Usually, this question or some version of it is intended to test the ethical boundaries. It is a way of asking what is "permissible" within the Christian rules about the expression of physical affection. What is the best response to this question?

We hope our vision expands your notion of intimate relationships and their expression. Such a vision does not begin by asking, "how far can we go," in a morally legalistic framework. Instead, it turns the question on its head. It asks: how far are *you* willing to go in living the mandate to love? How far are you willing to go in rooting your daily loving in the all-encompassing communion of God? How far will you go in honest communication? How much are you willing to stretch your heart in trust? How vulnerable and self-disclosing are you with your spouse or closest friends? How far will you go in helping to create psychic and spiritual safety in your relationships?

The Gospel vision challenges each of us to love deeply and generously. It does so positively by summoning us to responsible relationships that can be achieved only through intentional maturity. Most of us want relationships that will capture our imaginations and challenge our lives. We recognize that it is no longer feasible or possible to coerce people into ethical behavior with moral mandates and warnings. The true challenge of the Gospel is the depth and breadth of its promise and possibilities. The integral demands of Christian living — and they are truly demanding — flow much more from grace and possibility than from mere rules or restrictions.

Jesus reminds us that we are to give as we have been given to; that the measure we use to share our love will, in turn, be the measure with which we receive it (Lk 6:38; Mt 7:2; Mk 4:24). He also promises us that God does not "ration the Spirit" (Jn 3:34). The vision of Christian intimacy and communion, in other words, is rooted in abundance, not in scarcity or restriction. If we are willing to embrace this vision of relationships and its consequences, the harvest of love will be rich indeed.

Did his relationships with people make their lives a little less burdened? We do know the answers to these questions. The rest is mystery.

From Isolation to Communion

What can we learn about the meaning and vision of human intimacy from this brief profile of Jesus' relational life in the Gospels? We see here the human face of God's love reaching out in invitation and welcome. We find intimations of human loving that our popular cultural images cannot possibly address or comprehend. We hear whispers of our primal roots in the relational mystery of our Trinitarian God. We catch glimpses of our fundamental capacity to be open to relationships, the most obvious way in which we image God in this world. In reflecting on Jesus' way of loving and being present to people, we see revealed God's quiet, powerful dream for humanity: the divine longing to breach the walls of our fear and isolation with what Carl Rogers has described as "unconditional positive regard." We can, in short, learn of God's promise in Jesus to give us "a future with hope" (Jer 29:11).

Jesus speaks of this dream of mutuality and respect between human beings as the "reign of God." In the Synoptic Gospels, Jesus proclaims this saving presence as God's powerful love breaking into human life through ever-deepening and inclusive circles of relationships between persons (see Mk 3:31–35). In the other early Christian writings, especially those of the apostle Paul, this dream for restored human relationships is often referred to as *koinonia.* This inclusive term is translated in different ways, depending upon the circumstances in which it is used. Frequently, it is translated as "communion," suggesting perhaps the way in which redeemed human relationships mirror the divine mystery of Trinitarian love, whether in the church or in the outreach of its mission to all of humanity. On other occasions, it is translated as "partnership" referring to the hard-won companionship that emerges in ministry in the midst of doctrinal and institutional conflict (Gal 2:9). The Protestant community often understands this word as "fellowship" — that wide-ranging and inclusive binding force of compassion that flows from Gospel living. Finally, *koinonia* can also refer to the loving relationships between persons, whose tenderness and care concretize the wider reach of the community on a more immediate, interpersonal level.

It is within this overarching call to *koinonia* — sacred communion — that the affective bonds of friendship, the covenantal union of marriage, and the immense diversity of human mutuality derive their deeper and more inclusive meaning. This premise grounds a spirituality of intimacy within the Christian tradition. This far-reaching vision is the theological basis for an affirming and challenging approach to relationships; it is, in a manner of speaking, the mission statement for all forms of community.

31 Shaping a Theology of Compassion

You must be compassionate,
as God is compassionate.

—Luke 6:36

In Lewis Carroll's *Alice's Adventures in Wonderland,* the young girl tumbles down a rabbit's hole and finds herself in a strange, upside-down world. At one point in her adventures she comes to a place where several roads diverge. She stands before a confusing jumble of signs pointing in different directions.

"Would you tell me, please, which way I ought to go from here?" Alice asked the Cheshire cat who was sitting in a tree nearby.

"That depends a good deal on where you want to get to," the smiling feline said.

"I don't much care where," replied Alice.

"Then it doesn't matter which way you go," said the cat.[46]

Knowing where we want to go is of great consequence. Choosing the right road in the world of relationships is an urgent matter for us individually and as communities of faith and justice. We live in a world with an overwhelming array of options and pathways to explore. The roadmaps are complex and the signs along the way are confusing and often contradictory. We long to find a sense of direction about the unfolding purpose of our lives. In the realm of theology and spirituality we can describe this basic sense of direction as our *vision* — the encompassing perspective that grounds and compels our convictions and commitments.

In this book we've tried to reimage and reclaim this founding vision of the Judeo-Christian tradition regarding the meaning and purpose of sexuality. We can't do without a spiritual vision that guides our approach to relationships, sexuality, and human intimacy — like a roadmap for our physical terrain. "Without a vision," the Book of Proverbs reminds us, "the people perish" (Pr 11:14, our translation).

We are not speaking here of a vision unconnected to life — a purely abstract set of principles or a list of rules — but a way of seeing reality that embodies and shapes life's crucial issues. In other words, it is a vision with *implications:* spiritual and ethical consequences for our personal and interpersonal lives, as well as for our wider community. A vision's implications become clear in how it is *practiced* or lived out in the tapestry of our relationships. The wider community shows its vision, too, through its spiritual leadership, in helping its members live out the vision.

In Christian history, the process of encouraging, healing, and ministering to the community in its practice of the Gospel vision is known as *pastoral theology*. What is the central element of pastoral care? How can we tell if we are in a compassionate and welcoming community?

Pastoral ministry begins by accepting people where they are and listening respectfully to their stories, just as Jesus encountered the Samaritan woman at Jacob's well and invited her to share her life experience. It is a presence to be offered, not a program to be inflicted. The first task of ministry is to create a safe setting (see Jn 10:9) in which people can share their experience, unburden their hearts, and ask their questions. It involves tending to the real needs and best interests of those persons seeking our service. It presupposes respect for their dignity and makes room for their individual differences. Most of all, pastoral ministry values compassion above condemnation, invitation above exclusion, vision above rules; it calls persons to become their deepest and best selves as living images of God. Whether expressed in liturgical ritual, sacramental ministry, spiritual counseling, or social service, the core conditions of pastoral care include compassion, understanding, and fairness. Being "pastoral" involves a style of presence to God's people that encourages and heals as it accompanies them on their faith journey.

The life and ministry of Jesus offer us a timeless image of authentic spiritual care. His banquet tables are large enough for everyone and the deepest yearnings of people are given respect. Those being served are not in the first place the powerful and the crafty, but the poor and the outcast. Pastoral care is extended to those who don't usually have a place, who don't fit neatly into the acceptable categories. Jesus' image of the good shepherd suggests that the authentic minister has the well-being of the whole flock as a primary concern.

32 Our Dynamic Traditions

Revolution is not necessarily violent or negative. The discovery of radium by Madame Curie was a revolution in medicine and a signal benefit to humanity. Even so, revolution does not readily come to mind when we think of the papacy. Yet the Second Vatican Council was in the best sense a revolution, setting the Church on a new trajectory and profoundly touching all aspects of her life.

—Archbishop John R. Quinn

What Is Tradition?

Tradition refers to the ways in which the Christian community understands salvation history as it is fulfilled in the life and teaching of Jesus, and as it has become en-fleshed in the community's life over the centuries. Some of these traditions are perennial because of their clarity and foundational character. An example of this is the Ten Commandments in the Hebrew Scriptures. They were part of an ancient oral tradition before they were written down. They reflect, moreover, an ethical perspective that shares fundamental assumptions and similarities to many, if not most of the other great world religions. The Beatitudes, as found in Matthew and Luke, have a parallel role in the Christian tradition.

Other religious teachings and the ethical practices that embody them have not enjoyed the same clarity or unanimity, and have evolved over the centuries. For example, we need only consider how long it took Christianity to condemn slavery, even though respect for the human person is already contained in the teachings of the Hebrew prophets, the ministry and preaching of Jesus, and the practice of many early Christian communities. The emerging opposition of churches to the death penalty demonstrates the evolving understanding of reverence for life. The word "tradition" often evokes an image of ancient, constant practice. But this is not always the case. In actuality, tradition, like all of human experience, is a dynamic, living reality.

Sexuality and Its Evolving Tradition

Although most major religious traditions have long regarded the topic of human sexuality as the proper domain for moral teaching, there are several vital issues, such as sexual orientation, yet to be fully addressed. Most Christian denominations are struggling with how to balance moral clarity and continuity, on the one hand, with respect for the dignity of the person and inclusivity on the other. We know of no mainstream denomination that has been able to address this issue in contemporary times without considerable difficulty, controversy, and even polarizing division.

In the Catholic tradition, a collection of forty-two documents was published in 1978 under the title *Official Catholic Teachings: Love and Sexuality*. It contains what was then a compilation of the available guidance on the subject. While the editor of the collected documents presents them in a positive light, he nonetheless acknowledges that Catholic teaching on human sexuality can be perceived as "negative and limiting" because "more often than not, the popes developed their encyclicals and addresses [on sexuality] in response to the problems of their times."[47] Social crises thus affected the manner in which popes approached human relationships and intimacy, often motivating them to issue more warnings about sexuality than encouragements. Sexuality was viewed as a problem to be solved rather than a mystery to be explored and cherished. In an honest acknowledgment, the editor of the collected documents notes that the discussion of a topic such as sexuality can be "somewhat less than enriching" when "negation and apprehension are the point of departure."[48] In another candid admission, the editor reports that even the positive statements sink under a preponderance of the problematic and negative — not a helpful starting place for a pastoral theology of human sexuality.

Since the publication of these collected works, the Catholic Church has begun to take a more positive, affirming stance toward sexuality. The documents of the Second Vatican Council, the writings of Pope John Paul II, and the publications of various bishops' conferences have emphasized the giftedness of human sexuality, together with the responsibilities that such a gift demands. However, for some Catholics, disillusioned by the negative attitudes of the past, the change has been too little, too late. For them, the official teaching on human sexuality does not sufficiently reflect the life experiences of ordinary Catholics. As a result, many of these individuals look less to the church for guidance and more to their own consciences. Sadly, this often increases their sense of isolation and keeps them from contributing to the wisdom of the wider community.

Conversely, other Catholics consider any hint of change in church teaching in this sensitive area unnecessary and dangerous. These believers rely on what they perceive to be unchanging truths that provide continuity in the face of challenge. For them, a church that stands by long-held convictions is the only one that can offer effective guidance in matters of sexual morality.

Too much change for some, too little for others. This is the setting in which the task of discernment must unfold. Facing impatience on one side and fear on the other, the Christian community moves forward with the process of debate and dialogue. In the early centuries of Christianity the *sensus fidelium,* or the "sense of the faithful," played a more influential role in shaping the belief and practice of the church. This groundswell may seem dormant today, but it's there. Under the guidance of the Holy Spirit ordinary people travel the pathway of love. They fall in love and make life commitments. They pursue their dreams and carry out their responsibilities. They sacrifice their personal needs for those they love. In some circumstances their convictions lead them to emphasize the importance of caution and continuity. At other times, their discernment and commitment to relationships open up new perspectives on the mystery of love. However it is expressed, this "lived truth" of believing people has a vital role in shaping the future of human loving. Quietly, persistently, it is helping to carry the believing community toward the future with a collective wisdom that, in the end, will be faithful to the Gospel and inclusive of all our stories.

In one of the documents of the Second Vatican Council, we read this striking statement: "Their conscience is people's most secret core, and their sanctuary. There they are alone with God whose voice echoes in their depths."[49] These words give us a glimpse of how the Catholic Church, along with the other Christian denominations, is reclaiming the vital role of personal conscience for the contemporary believer. The document also reflects what we might describe as a sea change of understanding within the believing community. Under the leadership of Pope John XXIII, the church embraced religious pluralism and the inherent dignity of a person's conscience. The Second Vatican Council no longer portrays conscience as a passive receptacle for official teaching, but renews the church's earlier emphasis on this gift as integral to our moral and personal development.

But conscience is more than an inner voice of ethical discernment. In Spanish the words for conscience and consciousness are the same, and we prefer to approach conscience with this more inclusive perspective. We might describe it as *reflective experience* — the accumulated wisdom of our discernment, our choices, our mistakes, our courage, and our brokenness. It carries the unique stories that both express and shape our lives and relationships. "God created human beings," the old Hasidic saying goes, "because God loves stories." Our life stories, especially those that surround our yearning for love and intimacy, are the ways in which the divine Word becomes flesh in our lives. They are the unfinished symphonies of our soul's music, the paths we have walked, the learning we have done. As such, they represent our soul's unique wisdom, and are a valuable resource for the collective wisdom of the believing community.

Compassion Is a Listening Heart

Over the years, in our roles as psychotherapists, we have been practicing active listening as we receive the stories of our clients. In our roles as teachers, we join other lifelong learners in trying to articulate the vision and practice of communication skills, relationships, and human intimacy. Listening and teaching, receiving and responding, hearing and articulating: we feel a holy rhythm of presence, an invitation on a daily basis to "hear the word and to keep it," to carry the human journey with respect, and to enter the expansive cave of the human heart.

More recently, however, we've become aware that these two underlying rhythms of listening and teaching are not distinct ways of being, but simply two dimensions of one task. We have come to realize that teaching is inherently pastoral, for it is simply another way of listening—the willingness to be open to the mutual flow of ideas, convictions, and diverse perspectives in the shared pilgrimage toward truth. To teach is to enter the sacred ground of another's quest for understanding, to become a companion on the road to God. In the Gospels the word for a disciple is *mathetes,* literally, someone who "learns by listening." In this sense, we have come to understand our ministry as a call "to listen like a disciple" (Is 50:4 JB) to the seeking journey of our clients and other lifelong learners.

A listening heart is essential to pastoral ministry, especially when we receive life stories about relationships and the search for love. When the lawyer in Matthew's Gospel asks about the "great commandment," Jesus responds by quoting from the Book of Deuteronomy. This passage begins with the Hebrew word that has been, for thousands of years, an integral part of every Jewish person's memory and way of life: *Shema—Listen*, O Israel! This opening mandate is followed by the familiar words that we identify as the central ethos of the Judeo-Christian tradition: "You shall love the Lord your God with all your heart, with all your soul, and with all your mind. This is the greatest and first commandment. And a second is like it: You must love your neighbor as yourself" (Mt 22:37–39).

We believe that the opening mandate in this passage, *Listen*, is an integral dimension of the Great Commandment. The call to listen is not just an introduction to the law of love or a formulaic way of getting our attention. Listening is the threshold of loving, the primal invitation to healing journeys. It is the doorway to trust, the pathway to mutual understanding. Listening is the starting point, the background music, and the goal of pastoral care.

33 A New Sexual Vision

No one sews a piece of unshrunk cloth on an old cloak, for the patch pulls away from the cloak, and a worse tear is made. Neither is new wine put into old wineskins; otherwise, the skins burst, and the wine is spilled, and the skins are destroyed; but new wine is put into fresh wineskins, and so both are preserved.

—Matthew 9:16–17

Matthew and his community had good reason to remember the words of Jesus about patching old cloaks with unshrunken cloth, or putting new wine into old wineskins. As the early disciples embraced the implications of the Gospel, they found themselves living out his prophetic words in ways that they had neither chosen nor anticipated. The preaching of Jesus had stretched the worn fabric of Jewish religious tradition to the breaking point; and his boundary-breaking ministry, like new wine, did not rest easily in the cultural containers of his time.

As a result, the early Christian communities confronted the painful conflict that inevitably accompanies periods of historical upheaval. In their personal lives, in their families and synagogues, in their towns and villages, they faced the inevitable "tearing apart" of relationships and the "bursting" of familiar religious assumptions. In unsteady times, it is difficult to honor the past while carrying it forward into a more expansive future. How do we respect our wisdom tradition and still embody it in a more inclusive, compassionate way? This is the defining task of every prophetic movement. The premier model for this is, of course, Jesus himself. His preaching and ministry reclaimed the authentic roots of Judaism, even as he broke open the rigid boundaries that prevented the Gospel from flourishing in new lands and hearts. "Do not think that I have come to abolish the law or the prophets," he tells his followers. "I have come not to abolish but to fulfill" (Mt 5:17). In the same way, the early followers of the Way struggled to hold together the old and the new—to embrace continuity and change, uprooting and fulfilling, tradition and transformation.

Honoring the Past, Embracing the Future

As we begin a new century and a new millennium, our Christian communities face a similar challenge. We too are confronting painful conflicts and unresolved questions, especially regarding human sexuality. The experience of "tearing apart" and "bursting" is taking place both within our faith traditions and in our relationship to our culture. In our religious communities we are striving to honor the past while at the same time being open to new horizons. In relationship to our culture, we're trying to figure out what movements foster compassion and respect, and which are passing social fads.

There are two important tasks facing contemporary Christians with regard to human sexuality. The first is the internal agenda of revisiting our spiritual roots with the hope of finding common ground among our various denominations. The second is to convey this renewed vision to our culture, not only with words but, more importantly, in the embodied practice of our communities and our everyday relationships.

The first task of reclaiming our shared values around sexuality and relationships requires a spirit of respect and dialogue among our diverse communities. It also demands that we return to our spiritual roots with open hearts, that we approach the Gospel as good news for our time. This involves far more than merely "thinking outside the box." It is nothing less than a willingness to be converted, both personally and communally. It entails a commitment to find "new skins" — a fresh approach to old questions, a spirit of receptivity to the presence of the Holy Spirit in our lives.

The second challenge is discovering how to incarnate and live this renewed vision of relationships in today's world. In an age of increasing secularization, the dignity of persons is often reduced to market value, with the result that human sexuality becomes one more commodity in an economy that exploits the addictive needs and self-interest of its citizens. The call for responsible, covenantal relationships has little importance in the media or the public sector. One gets the impression that the only ethical question left in a world of recreational sex is that of consent.

What does Christianity have to say to such a culture? We can no longer rely on the authoritarian devices of fear, guilt, or shame to get people's attention or to change their behavior. Nor can we simply repeat creedal statements or ethical mandates from the past, assuming that old answers to sexual issues are adequate for today. Even in those instances where values are found to be truly timeless, expressing them in contemporary terminology, rather than the juridical language of the past, will give them greater credibility.

Clearly, we must move beyond a stance of judgment and condemnation to a spirit of affirmation and respect. We must let go of a narrow, fear-based morality while still challenging ourselves and our sisters and brothers to responsible loving. In short, we must honor our most authentic traditions regarding sexuality, and at the same time shape "new skins" — creative images and courageous practice — to embody that vision in today's world. Our religious traditions can serve as beacons of hope and heralds of transformation only if they invite such dialogue.

34 The Future of Human Loving

> *Write down the vision clearly upon the tablets, so that one can read it readily. For the vision still has its time, presses on to fulfillment, and will not disappoint.* —Habakkuk 2:2 (NAB)

How do we begin to shape new wineskins — fresh images and words — to help articulate the evolution of consciousness emerging around human sexuality? We face this challenge as individuals, as faith communities, and as a culture. It is a demanding task. All the same, the prophet Habakkuk reminds us that visions need to be written down. Evolving awareness seeks for words. Intuition craves expression.

In this final part of our book, we want to heed Habakkuk's challenge by trying to summarize what we see emerging in human loving and relationships. We therefore have to find words for unclear realities and name the themes revealed by our listening and ministry. To accomplish this purpose, we have developed a series of *vision statements*. These shifts in perspective won't give easy answers to specific sexual questions, but will describe the "new skins" for the wine of relational living in our time. They and this entire book invite you to further reflection, critical thinking, and dialogue.

VISION STATEMENTS: THE EMERGING SPIRITUALITY OF SEXUALITY

From a static to a *developmental* understanding of psychosexuality.

Until the scientific revolutions of the seventeenth and eighteenth centuries, it was assumed that human beings lived in a stable and unchanging cosmos. Although ancient people regularly faced dangers beyond their control, they nevertheless trusted in the presence of an unseen order. They believed that the earth was the center of a reasonably small and enduring universe. They spoke with ease of the eternal hills and the ever-flowing rivers; and at night they looked up into the familiar canopy of stars to guide their ships and determine their fates.

Contemporary science, on the other hand, reveals a universe billions of years old, more immense than we can imagine, and constantly evolving. In our world, evolution—the ongoing process of change—governs every aspect of our lives.

In the last half century this perspective of ongoing change has become familiar to us in the behavioral and social sciences. Developmental psychology has had a profound impact on our understanding of human life and growth. Concepts such as prenatal development, cognitive development, moral development, adult development, and faith development remind us that there is no magical point in human life where we can consider ourselves "finished." Rather, a dynamic force in the human soul compels us toward greater growth.

Theories of development have enhanced the earlier static approaches to sexual maturation, which saw puberty as the benchmark separating childhood from adulthood. While completion of secondary sex characteristics terminates *physiological* adolescence, these changes don't always include adult integration. We have come to understand that "growing up" involves far more than physical changes. Our biological maturing must also be accompanied by communication skills, by a deepening sense of moral responsibility, and by an emerging sense of creativity. This deeper integration involves a complex pattern of development that spans our entire lives.

The concept of development respects the unfinished character of our personalities and lives. It implies, in other words, a more compassionate understanding of *imperfection* — the psychic and spiritual wounds we inherit from our families and from the human condition, and the long journey, with God's grace, toward integration.

What happens when we graft the principles of psychosexuality onto religious moral teaching? How will our faith communities integrate their ethical vision with a developmental view of human growth? How can we challenge ourselves to forge responsible relationships and still make room for human failings? Perhaps, at the very least, we might be more compassionate in our use of language when identifying our continuing limitations. We must carry these vital questions and issues into the future.

From an emphasis on biological procreation to the more inclusive understanding of *generativity* as the goal of giving life.

The capacity for all life forms to propagate by having "offspring" is one of the most wondrous miracles in God's unfolding creation. Procreation is a gift and responsibility that the human community will continue to reverence and nurture.

However, biological reproduction is not the only way in which human persons give life. After a child has been born, loving parents continue to hold, feed, clothe, educate, and care for their daughters and sons. Rearing a child requires giving life beyond the biological to the emotional, spiritual, psychological, and cognitive dimensions. Cutting an umbilical cord does not end the process of giving life, but rather opens up new ways in which life will be experienced between parent and child and the wider community.

But the call to give life is not just for parents; it is for every human person. It is a responsibility larger than procreativity, a vocation that transcends our state in life, our gender, our age, or our sexual orientation. This vital area of Christian spirituality needs further reflection and insight. How is each of us called to be a life-giver? How are we generative in our friendships, our communities, and our places of work? What is the creative passion with which we express our unique gifts? If we are parents, how do we continue to give life after our children have grown? How might a broader understanding of "giving life" influence the specifically genital aspects of our sexuality? And how might it impact our approach to the rainforests and rivers, the air and the soil?

> From speaking of sexuality primarily as genital behavior to expanding it to include *energy for relationships.*

In Western culture, sexuality has become virtually synonymous with genital behavior. In the world of advertising, sexual images sell everything from cosmetics to lawn furniture. We have become so familiar with provocative scenes in our films and sitcoms that we become numb to their impact on our emotions and inner lives. The graphic lyrics in popular music trivialize physical intimacy and in many instances link it explicitly to violence and to the exploitation of women. For most people in our society, sexuality has only the one-dimensional reality of genital expression.

Until recently, most of our religious traditions also tended to approach sexuality primarily in terms of its biological role in the procreation of children. Within marital commitment, physical intimacy was understood as a necessary — and even holy — means to perpetuate the human community. It was only after marriage evolved from the social exchange of property to an affirmation of mutuality that religious traditions began to recognize the emotional, psychic, and spiritual dimensions of sexuality.

The renewed emphasis on mutual love in marriage is a significant step forward. But this perspective on the meaning and purpose of sexuality still limits it primarily to marriage. As we have seen throughout these chapters, sexuality needs to be understood even more widely as *energy for relationships* — an "aptitude for forming bonds of communion with others" that begins to unfold in our lives even before we are born. No matter what our age, gender, orientation, or state in life, each of us is sexual. Every person is gifted with divine eros, with a restless desire for life and relationships, with a passion for creativity and the gift of self. Every human person wants beauty, mutuality, and friendship. Each of us seeks the face of the beloved and, ultimately, the countenance of the living God.

From suspicion of sexuality to its *reverence and celebration* as sacred energy.

"The eye is the lamp of the body," Jesus tells his followers. "So, if your eye is healthy, your whole body will be full of light; but if your eye is unhealthy, your whole body will be full of darkness" (Mt 6:22–23). This is the Gospel's way of reminding us that our outlook on life makes a difference. The attitude of our minds and hearts profoundly influences what we see in the people, events, and circumstances of our daily living. Jesus' earthy proverb is particularly true when applied to human sexuality. The health of our "inner eye" will strongly determine the response of our heart, the patterns of our conversation, even the behaviors and choices of our life journey.

In the course of history, many religious traditions looked upon human sexuality with fear and suspicion. If, in addition to these religious messages, we grew up in a family where verbal or nonverbal attitudes toward sexuality generated shame or guilt, we will struggle painfully to understand how human passion can be a gift or a blessing.

If we find ourselves suspicious about human sexuality, we will experience it more as a threat than a gift. The "lamp of our body" will be filled with darkness. A review of the documents on sexuality for most mainline Christian denominations reveals that they usually open with positive introductory descriptions of sexuality as sacred and part of God's good creation. Then they quickly move to a discussion of the dangers and misuses of the sexual appetite — usually identified more as specific sexual acts outside of marriage, than examples of violation and mistreatment of people. Rules to prevent the sinful use of sex usually form the bulk of these documents, with little expansion of the positive statements, despite their power and insight.

What would happen if our churches gave more space to the beauty, goodness, and grace of sexuality, focusing their teaching more on the meaning and expression of healthy, faithful human intimacy? What difference would it make if long paragraphs devoted to the relationship between sexuality and justice replaced the rules and warnings about sex outside of marriage?

While it's healthy to remember sexuality's pains and risks, a liberating spirituality ought not begin with a list of dangers and punishments. The sacred energy that is part of falling in love and giving birth deserves first to be celebrated, so that it can also be protected and cherished.

The word "celebrate" is related to the Greek term *heortazo,* to have a festival. In Latin, *celebrare* implies that something is worth honoring. Indeed, the "rites of loving" are sacramental ways of honoring those gifts that are most sacred to us. Whether it is the spontaneous, simple affection between friends, a quiet conversation over dinner, or the total self-gift of sexual intercourse, each of these human rituals *honors* what is already a shared spiritual reality. Celebration is built into every expression of sexual energy. How can a renewed vision of human sexuality create a sense of celebration and still summon us to values that reverence and respect people?

From sex education for youth to *psychosexual formation* for lifelong learners.

In many schools and religious education programs "sex education" consists of a presentation, a class, or a video on subjects related to biological reproduction, the physiological changes associated with puberty, and information on sexually transmitted diseases. In public schools these programs generally focus on *information* that is considered ethically neutral and nonreligious. Private schools and religious education programs tend to focus less on information and more on moral *rules*. In both instances, the foundational values related to emotional intelligence, relationship skills, and the meaning of intimacy usually get less time and attention. In our experience, the two most important areas of preparing young people for adult loving — namely, communication skills and friendship formation — are often missing altogether.

Most parents know that if they delay discussions about sexuality until puberty, they miss an opportunity to guide the early formation of their children's attitudes and values. They also recognize that having a single "sex talk" with a ten-year-old no longer qualifies as effective sex education for a child. Teachers likewise understand that classroom lectures about anatomy and physiology, thirty-minute videos on reproduction, and teen chastity workshops are not enough to prepare a young person for the complex world of relationships.

Given the groundswell of concern about sexuality, our faith communities have a prophetic opportunity to change this situation for the better. The challenge for the future is to reimagine "sex education" as something more than a cautionary program for adolescents, and to see it instead as "psychosexual education" for a lifetime. Many faith communities have already developed models of psychosexual formation that embrace all stages of our growth. Just as eating, sleeping, and praying are constant rhythms throughout our lives, so is psychosexual formation — the ongoing need to keep growing in our understanding of love and our capacity for giving life.

A renewed theology of human sexuality must be young enough to engage children, open enough to be taken seriously by teens, credible enough to challenge young adults, seasoned enough to understand the needs of all of those in the middle years, wise enough for the elderly, and sufficiently compassionate to embrace all of us over a lifetime.

From dualism to *integration* as the framework for a spirituality of human sexuality.

Body-soul. Flesh-spirit. Secular-sacred. These conceptual polarities are part of the philosophical system broadly understood as *dualism*, discussed in earlier chapters. This ancient view of reality arose, in part, as an attempt to account for the presence of evil in our world. It usually involves a theory of cosmic conflict between light and darkness, good and evil, spirit and flesh. Its long and complicated history reaches as far back as Zoroaster, the Manichees, and ancient Eastern cosmogonies. It resurfaces in diverse forms ranging from Docetism, Gnosticism, and neo-Platonism in the early church, to the Albigensians and Cathars of the Middle Ages and to the Jansenists in more recent times.

These various strands of philosophy share some central beliefs. They all hold that the human person has a *dual* nature consisting of a body (matter or flesh) and a spirit (mind or soul). Flesh is considered transitory at best, and even regarded as evil by some dualists. The mind, or knowledge, is a higher value and more "real" than flesh. Although Christianity is inherently incarnational in its vision and spirituality — and therefore opposed to a dualistic explanation — this perspective reappeared in various forms at different times in history. There is evidence that Paul and other first-century authors were already combating forms of dualism in their communities of faith. St. Augustine, regarded as perhaps the most influential Christian teacher on sexual morals, was himself a Manichean Gnostic prior to his conversion to Christianity. Some scholars maintain that Augustine never quite got beyond his early dualism, particularly about sexuality, even after his embrace of Christianity.

Much of the body-soul division in Christian teaching — in which the body was considered less pure than the soul — can be traced to a spirituality seeking to escape the human condition. Though we are gradually moving beyond these unfortunate dualisms, their lingering guilt and spiritual anguish have left scars in many believers. How do we move beyond the belief that bodies are less noble than souls? How can we reclaim a spirituality that affirms the goodness of our flesh? What will enable us to trust that our passion for life and relationships has God as its source and destiny? A renewed spirituality of human sexuality can do nothing less.

From identifying sexual sin as illicit genital pleasure to recognizing it as the *violation of persons.*

A dualistic understanding of the human person has left behind the notion that there is something inherently "evil" about sexual feelings and genital pleasure. In the ethical consciousness of many believers, "sexual sin" means any form of sexual arousal outside marital commitment. How did this situation arise? Over the centuries the ethical concerns of Christianity gradually shifted from the earlier biblical concern for justice in relationships to a private morality preoccupied with the "disordered" nature of sexual desire. The result of these attitudes was a highly negative, juridical morality that focused on "illicit pleasure" with little regard for the quality of relationships or the social dimensions of the Gospel.

Where, then, is the real locus of "sexual sin"? It is not the experience of pleasure that is sinful, but rather the violation of persons. Every sexual experience has an intrinsic relational and spiritual quality. But if sexual behavior is irresponsible, if it violates a covenantal commitment or is forced on another person — even if this happens within the "legitimate" bonds of marriage — this exploitation destroys the relationship and distorts the intrinsic meaning of loving. This conviction challenges the belief that marriage, in and of itself, makes sexual intercourse sacred, and invites us to think about what really provides the "holy ground" for genital sharing.

In contemporary spirituality, the unhealthy preoccupation with illicit pleasure is being replaced with a more person-centered ethic based on mutual respect in our relationships. Sexual morality is reclaiming its roots in biblical justice as the call to restore right relationships. A Lutheran pastor at a national ministry conference recalled the many sermons he heard as an adolescent warning against premarital sex. "But, I never once heard a sermon on domestic violence or sexual abuse," he reported. His experience was echoed by one of our Catholic graduate theology students who remarked that, "The church has powerful things to say on social justice, but this continues to be one of the best-kept secrets in the church. I wish we would give it a lot more press. This is where the focus of classes on morality ought to be."

What steps can our churches take to confront the abuse of power and the sexual violation of persons? Do sins against relationship take place only in the bedroom or do they also exist in the boardroom? Are they primarily private experiences of genital pleasure or are they also forms of systemic violence — institutional attitudes and decisions that erode the dignity of people? This growing concern for the violation of persons, both by individuals and by institutions, is refocusing the meaning and scope of sexual morality.

From patriarchy to *partnership* as the philosophical mindset for determining sexual and gender ethics.

Many men distrust discussions about patriarchy, which seem to implicate all male persons in a long-standing conspiracy to dominate women. They point out, and rightly so, that dominating other people is not gender specific. It is important to distinguish between *patriarchy* as a historical, social reality from what might be called the *dominating personality*.

In many parts of our world, there are hopeful signs of movement toward greater male-female equality.

But while there's a lot of talk about mutuality and collaboration, the promises often fail to match performance. In spite of equal opportunity policies and equality belief statements, male dominance is still a reality in many areas of human relationships. Again, we don't mean to imply that most males are dominating; rather, we recognize that leadership in most institutions, governments, and organizations is still under the collective control of males. As a society, we continue to wrestle with this reality and its implications. We have seen the rise of many forms of feminism, witnessed the emergence of parallel male movements, and supported women as they try to balance motherhood with a professional career. We have read the books, joined the support groups, debated inclusive language in our liturgies, listened to the talk shows, walked the picket lines, and attended seminars. But true gender partnership in our world still seems to elude us.

The role of women remains an especially sensitive one in our churches. While our Christian teaching strongly emphasizes the fundamental equality of women and men, the struggle to implement this vision still continues, in many instances with a great deal of resistance. Rooted in the Christian teaching on the equality and dignity of all people, the call for gender justice will continue to challenge us in the future.

From sexual abstinence to *reverence in relationships* as the hallmark of psychosexual wholeness and holiness.

Is one Christian vocation more sacred than another? Does the commitment to live without genital expression please God more than marriage? Although the church has not taught that sexual abstinence is essential to holiness, it has maintained that celibacy represents a "higher state of life" than marriage. In the minds of many older Christians, Catholics in particular, even the sexual expressiveness in marriage is somehow "tainted" or at least less noble than a lifetime of sexual restraint. The Catholic Church's emphasis on celibacy for priests and members of religious orders has given the impression that sexual abstinence is a kind of Catholic "litmus test" for authentic holiness.

On the other hand, the central commandment — the single, persuasive sign of discipleship that Jesus has given us — is as simple as it is direct: "By this everyone will know that you are my disciples, if you love one another" (Jn 13:35). He speaks of love not in terms of genital abstinence, but as a radical respect for the other and the willingness to lay down one's life for one's friends. He focuses on the mandates of the heart: forgiveness of one's enemies, patience, care for the poor, and compassion for sinners. He does not "abolish the law" but places greater emphasis on its underlying spirit. In practice, he asks one thing of his followers: that we have the same compassion for one another that God has for all of us. By his life and preaching, he gives us examples of authentic love stories: gazing out over Jerusalem, feeling the longing of a mother hen for her chicks; making a picnic for hungry crowds on a hillside; having a long conversation with a foreign woman at a well; sitting in a house with his closest friends gathered about him in a circle; and crying when his friend, Lazarus, died.

Whatever words they use to articulate it, most Christians today believe that reverence in relationships, the kind that comes from playful, committed, joyous, and disciplined loving, is the central call of their faith. It is also the most pressing mandate for a Christian spirituality of human sexuality. Our faith communities will necessarily hold in memory both the innate giftedness as well as the potential brokenness of human sexuality as we continue to renew our spirituality of relationships.

35 The Promise of Tomorrow

> *For surely I know the plans I have for you, says the Lord, plans for your welfare and not for harm, to give you a future with hope.*
>
> —Jeremiah 29:11

We have been describing a quiet but sweeping transformation taking place in our experience and understanding of human sexuality. What are the implications of these shifts in vision? In what way do they describe emerging convictions about human sexuality? Where are they being named and lived in our families, our friendships, and our communities of faith?

Lived Experience and an Emerging Story

On one level these thematic statements summarize what is already stirring in people's lives and relationships — in their prayer and conversation, in their offices and backyards, in their classrooms and discussion groups, on their dates and around the kitchen table. They are emerging as quiet convictions from teenagers, college students, pastoral ministers, and professional colleagues. Usually, they are named in ordinary images, halting phrases, unfinished sentences, by people who are young and old, male and female, gay and straight, married and single, divorced and widowed, celibate by choice and celibate by circumstance.

Our vision statements also reflect the current spirituality and pastoral practice of many congregations, parishes, and other intentional communities of faith. We've picked up threads of this quiet shift from the dialogue and debate currently taking place among Methodists, Presbyterians, Unitarian Universalists, Lutherans, Catholics, Congregationalists, Episcopalians, the United Church of Christ, American Baptists, and other denominations. Courageous choices of persons like Jimmy Carter, who withdrew from his faith tradition because of its patriarchal stance toward women, as well as countless others with similar concerns about love and justice, take risks that demonstrate the urgency of sexual and relational issues in contemporary life.

On another level, these changes in the state-of-the-question predict a vision still to be en-fleshed, a promise waiting to be fulfilled. They are more reflective than conclusive. They point to directions, not details — to stirrings in the human heart and imagination that still need further clarification. As early as 1934, Teilhard de Chardin wrote of a quiet, spiritual groundswell beginning to stir in human consciousness, pointing toward an evolution of human relationships. In our contemporary world, perhaps these horizon shifts reflect our growing desire "to harness for God the energies of love."[50]

Standing at a New Horizon

Finally, we want to emphasize that these vision statements are not new or disconnected from the Judeo-Christian tradition. Rather, they rearticulate the core values of our heritage for a new time. They have been quietly taking shape in the collective human conscience for hundreds, perhaps thousands of years. They are as old as Isaiah's pleas for freedom on behalf of the downtrodden and as close to our Christian tradition as Jesus' compassion for the woman taken in adultery. Like the householder described in the Gospel of Matthew, we are called to bring out of our storehouse both what is old and what is new (Mt 13:52).

With these vision statements, we hope to illuminate the changing perspectives and deeper understandings coming to light in our time. They presuppose that the vantage point of our experience influences how we interpret what we see. For example, when we stand at the edge of the ocean on a fog-shrouded day, we can see the horizon only dimly, if at all. But we still know that the ocean is there. When the fog begins to lift, we see farther. Yet, even on a clear day when the sun makes the waves sparkle and the horizon seems to go on forever, we recognize that there is a vastness and a depth that we cannot see.

We can apply this same spirit of open interpretation to the mystery of human relationships. When we choose to love, we enter a horizon without limits, an ocean of infinite depth. There is always more to our restlessness and the desires of our hearts than we can put into words. And there is more to the stirring of our passions and the circles of our loving than we can ever comprehend. Perhaps God created our sexuality as an expansive longing, so our hearts would never give up on the quest for love.

Notes

1. Unless otherwise noted, Scripture quotations are from the New Revised Standard Version (NRSV). Other abbreviations: JB (Jerusalem Bible), NAB (New American Bible), Phillips (J. B. Phillips Translation).

2. The Pastoral Constitution on the Role of the Church in the Modern World, *Vatican Council II: The Basic Sixteen Documents,* ed. Austin Flannery (Northport, N.Y.: Costello Publishing Co., 1996), no. 1 (emphasis added).

3. John Ayto, *Dictionary of Word Origins* (New York: Arcade Publishing, 1993), 470.

4. Ibid.

5. Vincent J. Genovesi, *In Pursuit of Love: Catholic Morality and Human Sexuality,* 2d ed. (Collegeville, Minn.: Liturgical Press, 1996), 132.

6. Brian Swimme and Thomas Berry, *The Universe Story: From the Primordial Flaring Forth to the Ecozoic Era — Celebration of the Unfolding of the Cosmos* (San Francisco: HarperSanFranciso, 1992), 5.

7. Brian Swimme, *The Universe Is a Green Dragon: A Cosmic Creation Story* (Santa Fe, N.Mex.: Bear & Company, 1995), 43–52.

8. Lorna Green, *Earth Age: A New Vision of God, the Human, and the Earth* (New York: Paulist Press, 1994), 117.

9. Deborah Tannen, *The Argument Culture: Moving from Debate to Dialogue* (New York: Random House, 1998).

10. See Daniel Goleman, *Emotional Intelligence: Why It Can Matter More Than IQ* (New York: Bantam Books, 1995).

11. Walter Brueggemann, *The Prophetic Imagination* (Philadelphia: Fortress Press, 1978), 13–27.

12. R. Michael, J. Gagnon, E. Laumann, and G. Kolata, *Sex in America: A Definitive Survey* (New York: Little, Brown, 1994), 25ff.

13. Douglas Coupland, *Life after God* (New York: Simon and Schuster, 1995), 359.

14. Daphne Merkin, "The Women in the Balcony: On Rereading the Song of Songs," in *Out of the Garden: Women Writers on the Bible,* ed. Christina Buchman and Celina Spiegel (New York: Fawcett Columbine, 1995), 249–51.

15. For example, Catherine LaCugna, *God for Us: The Trinity in Christian Life* (San Francisco: HarperSanFrancisco, 1991). Also Michael Downey, *Altogether Gift: A Trinitarian Spirituality* (Maryknoll, N.Y.: Orbis Books, 2000).

16. Loren Eiseley, *The Immense Journey: An Imaginative Naturalist Explores the Mysteries of Man and Nature* (New York: Vintage Books, 1946). See also Swimme and Berry, *The Universe Story.*

17. Pierre Teilhard de Chardin, *The Human Phenomenon,* new edition and translation by Sarah Appleton-Weber (Portland, Ore.: Sussex Academic Press, 1999); see especially 11–36. See also James Conlon, *Earth Story, Sacred Story* (Mystic, Conn.: Twenty-Third Publications, 1994), 7–56.

18. Timothy Ferris, *Coming of Age in the Milky Way* (New York: William Morrow, 1988), 381–88.

19. Caroline J. Simon, *The Disciplined Heart: Love, Destiny, and Imagination* (Grand Rapids, Mich.: William B. Eerdmans, 1997).

20. Anon., *The Cloud of Unknowning and the Book of Privy Counseling,* ed. William Johnston (Garden City, N.Y.: Image Books, 1973), 66.

21. Joyce Carol Oates, *Blonde* (New York: Ecco Press/Harper Collins, 2000).

22. Deirdre Donahue, "Uncovering 'Blonde' Roots: Novelist Oates Explores Marilyn's Lost Norma Jean," *USA Today,* April 10, 2000, 1D.

23. *Sex in America,* 230ff.

24. For many of the insights in this section, we are indebted to

Paul Avis, *Eros and the Sacred* (Harrisburg, Pa., Wilton, Conn.: Morehouse Publishing, 1989), 128–37.

25. Dionysius, *The Divine Names* and *The Mystical Theology,* trans C. E. Rolt (London: SPCK, 1940), 101, as cited in Avis, *Eros and the Sacred,* 133.

26. Anders Nygren, *Agape and Eros* (New York: Harper and Row, 1969).

27. Frederick Buechner, *Wishful Thinking: A Theological ABC* (New York: Harper and Row), 53.

28. Paul Ricoeur, *The Symbolism of Evil* (Boston: Beacon Press, 1967).

29. *Catechism of the Catholic Church,* 2d ed. (Washington, D.C.: United States Catholic Conference, 2000), no. 2346.

30. National Conference of Catholic Bishops, *Human Sexuality: A Catholic Perspective for Education and Lifelong Learning* (Washington, D.C.: United States Catholic Conference, 1990).

31. It was our original intention to cite examples from a variety of mainline religious traditions throughout this book. However, it became evident that such extensive documentation would burden the reader with too much footnoted material. Instead, we encourage our readers to consult the documents on human sexuality from their own faith traditions. Frequently, this information can be obtained on a website or by contacting a church, synagogue, or place of worship.

32. *Catechism of the Catholic Church,* no. 2332.

33. Ibid., no. 1776 (male pronouns changed to plural for inclusivity)

34. Ibid., no. 1779 (female pronouns in parenthesis for inclusivity)

35. Spencer A. Rathus, Jeffrey S. Nevid, Lois Fichner-Rathus, *Human Sexuality in a World of Diversity,* 4th ed. (Boston: Allyn and Bacon, 2000), 212–21.

36. For a more extensive biblical reflection on intimacy see our book, *Your Sexual Self: Pathway to Authentic Intimacy* (Notre Dame, Ind.: Ave Maria Press, 1992), 153 ff.

37. Dag Hammarsjköld, *Markings,* trans. L. Sjober and W. H. Auden (New York: Ballantine Books, 1983), 58.

38. Although we describe and apply them in different ways, we are indebted to Daniel L. Richards, Ph.D., for these three images of intimacy in a presentation he gave entitled "Co-Dependency in Males," 1991.

39. Kathryn Dindia and Mike Allen, "Sex Differences in Self-Disclosure: A Meta-Analysis," *Psychological Bulletin* 12 (1992): 106–24.

40. Joseph Campbell, *The Power of Myth,* with Bill Moyers (New York: Doubleday, 1988) 7, emphasis added.

41. Dorothy Day, "On Pilgrimage," *Catholic Worker,* July/ August, 1971, 2, 8.

42. *Catechism of the Catholic Church,* no. 2332 (emphasis added).

43. *Vatican Council II: The Basic Sixteen Documents,* Gaudium et Spes, no. 24.

44. Pope John Paul II, *The Theology of the Body: Human Love in the Divine Plan* (Boston: Pauline Books & Media, 1997), 78, emphasis added.

45. Daphne Merkin, "The Women in the Balcony: On Rereading the Song of Songs," *Out of the Garden: Women Writers on the Bible,* ed. Christina Buchman and Celina Spiegel (New York: Fawcett Columbine, 1995), 244–45.

46. Lewis Carroll, *Alice's Adventures in Wonderland* (New York: Penguin Signet Classic, 1960), 64.

47. *Official Catholic Teachings: Love and Sexuality,* ed. Odile M. Liebard (Wilmington, N.C.: Consortium Books, 1978), xvii.

48. Ibid., vii.

49. *Vatican Council II: The Basic Sixteen Documents,* Gaudium et Spes, no. 16.

50. Pierre Teilhard de Chardin, "The Evolution of Chastity," in *Toward the Future,* ed. and trans. Rene Hague (New York: Harcourt, Brace, Jovanovich, 1975), 60–87.

Select Bibliography

Anon., *The Cloud of Unknowing and the Book of Privy Counseling.* Ed. William Johnston. Garden City, N.Y.: Image Books, 1973.

Avis, Paul. *Eros and the Sacred.* Harrisburg, Pa., Wilton, Conn.: Morehouse Publishing, 1989.

Bailie, Gil. *Violence Unveiled: Humanity at the Crossroads.* New York: Crossroad, 1995.

Boswell, John. *Christianity, Social Tolerance, and Homosexuality: Gay People in Western Europe from the Beginning of the Christian Era to the Fourteenth Century.* Chicago and London: University of Chicago Press, 1980.

Brown, Peter. *The Body and Society: Men, Women, and Sexual Renunciation in Early Christianity.* New York: Columbia University Press, 1988.

Brueggemann, Walter. *The Prophetic Imagination.* Philadelphia: Fortress Press, 1978.

Büchmann, Christina, and Celina Spiegel, eds. *Out of the Garden: Women Writers on the Bible.* New York: Fawcett Columbine, 1995.

Cahill, Lisa Sowle. *Sex Gender, and Christian Ethics.* Cambridge University Press, 1966.

Carnes, Patrick. *Don't Call It Love.* New York: Bantam Books, 1991.

Carnes, Patrick, D. Delmonico, E. Griffin. *In the Shadow of the Net: Breaking Free of Compulsive Online Sexual Behavior.* Center City, Minn.: Hazelden, 2001.

Carroll, Lewis. *Alice's Adventures in Wonderland.* New York: Penguin Signet Classic, 1960.

Catechism of the Catholic Church. 2d ed. Libreria Editrice Vaticana, 1994; United States Catholic Conference, 1997.

Collins, Raymond F. *Sexual Ethics and the New Testament: Behavior and Belief.* New York: Crossroad, 2000.

Conlon, James. *Earth Story, Sacred Story.* Mystic, Conn.: Twenty-Third Publications, 1994.

Countryman, L. William. *Dirt, Greed and Sex: Sexual Ethics in the New Testament and Their Implications for Today.* Philadelphia: Fortress Press, 1988.

Coupland, Douglas. *Life After God.* New York: Simon and Schuster, 1995.

Downey, Michael. *Altogether Gift: A Trinitarian Spirituality.* Maryknoll, N.Y.: Orbis Books, 2000.

Eiseley, Loren. *The Immense Journey: An Imaginative Naturalist Explores the Mysteries of Man and Nature.* New York: Vintage Books, 1946.

Ferder, Fran. *Words Made Flesh: Scripture, Psychology and Human Communication.* Notre Dame, Ind.: Ave Maria Press, 1986.

Ferder, Fran, and John Heagle. *Partnership: Women and Men in Ministry.* Notre Dame, Ind.: Ave Maria Press, 1989.

———. *Your Sexual Self: Pathway to Authentic Intimacy.* Notre Dame, Ind.: Ave Maria Press, 1992.

Ferris, Timothy. *Coming of Age in the Milky Way.* New York: William Morrow and Company, 1988.

Flannery, Austin, O.P., ed. *Vatican Council II: A Completely Revised Translation in Inclusive Language.* Northport, N.Y.: Costello Publishing Company, 1996.

Fortune, Marie M. *Is Nothing Sacred?: When Sex Invades the Pastoral Relationship.* San Francisco: Harper and Row, 1989.

———. *Sexual Violence: The Unmentionable Sin.* New York: Pilgrim Press, 1983.

Fox, Thomas C. *Sexuality and Catholicism.* New York: George Braziller, 1995.

Genovesi, Vincent J. *In Pursuit of Love: Catholic Morality and Human Sexuality.* 2d ed. Collegeville, Minn.: Liturgical Press, 1996.

Green, Lorna. *Earth Age: A New Vision of God, the Human and the Earth.* New York: Paulist Press, 1994.

Gudorf, Christine E. *Body, Sex, and Pleasure: Reconstructing Christian Sexual Ethics.* Cleveland: Pilgrim Press, 1994.

Guindon, Andre. *The Sexual Language: An Essay in Moral Theology.* Ottawa: University of Ottawa Press, 1976.

Heagle, John. *Jesus: Divine and Human; Reflections from Matthew.* Intersections Small Group Series. Minneapolis: Augsburg Fortress, 1995.

Irvine, Janice M. *Sexuality Education across Cultures: Working with Differences.* San Francisco: Jossey-Bass, 1995.

John Paul II, Pope. *The Theology of the Body: Human Love in the Divine Plan.* Boston: Pauline Books and Media, 1997.

Jung, Patricia Beattie, Mary E. Hunt, and Radhika Balakrishnan, eds. *Good Sex.* New Brunswick, N.J., and London: Rutgers University Press, 2001.

Kennedy, Eugene. *The Unhealed Wound: The Church and Human Sexuality.* New York: St. Martin's Press, 2001.

Kosnik, Anthony, et al. *Human Sexuality: New Directions in American Catholic Thought; A Study Commissioned by The Catholic Theological Society of America.* New York: Paulist Press, 1977.

LaCugna, Catherine. *God for Us: The Trinity in Christian Life.* San Francisco: Harper, 1991.

Liebard, Odile M., ed. *Official Catholic Teachings: Love and Sexuality.* Wilmington, N.C.: McGrath Publishing Company, 1978.

Liuzzi, Peter J., O.Carm. *With Listening Hearts: Understanding the Voices of Lesbian and Gay Catholics.* New York and Mahwah, N.J.: Paulist Press, 2001.

Michael, Robert T., John H. Gagnon, Edward O. Laumann, and Gina Kolata. *Sex in America: A Definitive Survey.* Boston, New York: Little, Brown and Company, 1994.

National Conference of Catholic Bishops (NCCB). *Human Sexuality: A Catholic Perspective for Education and Lifelong*

Learning. Washington, D.C.: United States Catholic Conference, 1990.

Nelson, James B. *Between Two Gardens: Reflections on Sexuality and Religious Experience.* New York: Pilgrim Press, 1983.

———. *Embodiment: An Approach to Sexuality and Christian Theology.* Minneapolis: Augsburg Publishing House, 1978.

Nelson, James B., and Sandra P. Longfellow, eds. *Sexuality and the Sacred: Sources for Theological Reflection.* Louisville: Westminster John Knox Press, 1994.

Nygren, Anders. *Agape and Eros.* New York: Harper and Row, 1969.

Oates, Joyce Carol. *Blonde.* New York: Ecco Press/HarperCollins, 2000.

Oliver, Mary Anne McPherson. *Conjugal Spirituality: The Primacy of Mutual Love in Christian Tradition.* Kansas City: Sheed and Ward, 1994.

Rathus, Spencer A., Jeffrey S. Nevid, and Lois Fichner-Rathus. *Human Sexuality in a World of Diversity.* 4th ed. Boston: Allyn and Bacon, 2000.

Ricoeur, Paul. *The Symbolism of Evil.* Boston: Beacon Press, 1967.

Rolheiser, Ronald. *The Holy Longing: The Search for a Christian Spirituality.* New York: Doubleday, 1999.

Scroggs, Robin. *The New Testament and Homosexuality: Contextual Background for Contemporary Debate.* Philadelphia: Fortress Press, 1983.

Simon, Caroline J. *The Disciplined Heart: Love, Destiny, and Imagination.* Grand Rapids, Mich.: William B. Eerdmans, 1997.

Somé, Sobonfu. *The Spirit of Intimacy: Ancient Teachings in the Ways of Relationships.* New York: William Morrow & Co., 1999.

Swimme, Brian. *The Universe Is a Green Dragon: A Cosmic Creation Story.* Santa Fe, N.Mex.: Bear and Company, 1995.

Swimme, Brian, and Berry, Thomas. *The Universe Story: From the Primordial Flaring Forth to the Ecozoic Era—A Celebration of the Unfolding of the Cosmos.* San Francisco: Harper, 1992.

Tannen, Deborah. *The Argument Culture: Moving From Debate to Dialogue.* New York: Random House, 1998.

Trible, Phyllis. *God and the Rhetoric of Sexuality.* Philadelphia: Fortress Press, 1978.

Walker, Alice. *The Color Purple.* New York: Simon and Schuster, Pocket Books, 1982.

Whitehead, Evelyn Eaton, and Whitehead, James D. *Wisdom of the Body: Making Sense of Our Sexuality.* New York: Crossroad, 2002.

Acknowledgments

This book reflects the shared wisdom and support of many groups and individuals, each of whom care deeply about relationships and believe that a renewed vision of human sexuality is not only necessary but possible. We are especially grateful to our families, friends, and colleagues who have lived what this book is about — who have given us love and life — and sustained us with laughter, affection, and prayer.

We are profoundly indebted to our graduate students in the School of Theology and Ministry (and the earlier SUMORE Program) at Seattle University, who, for seventeen years, have shared their vision of a renewed theology of human sexuality with us. Their questions, challenges, and insights are integral to these chapters.

Those who have participated in our workshops, retreats, classes, and conferences have also helped shape our writing. It has been inspiring to work with women and men in ministry who listen to the everyday concerns about sexuality from the "folks in the pews." We have found our work at Retreats International at the University of Notre Dame; the

Los Angeles Religious Education Congress; the Intercommunity Peace and Justice Center, Seattle, Washington; and the Marianella Center in Dublin, Ireland, to be especially rich sources of inspiration and learning.

For more than twenty years, we have been privileged to work with many religious orders of women and men, Catholic diocesan clergy, and Protestant ministers in a variety of settings. The vision we share has provided continuous enlightenment and energy. We are especially indebted to the Sisters of Providence, Mother Joseph Province, Seattle/Spokane; the Franciscan Friars of Santa Barbara, California; the BVMs, Dubuque, Iowa; the Marianites of Holy Cross, New Orleans; the Marist Brothers of Australia; the CSJP's of Seattle, Washington; the Maryknoll Sisters, New York; the Benedictine Sisters of Eau Claire, Wisconsin; the Jesuits of several American Provinces; seminarians at the American College in Louvain, Belgium, and the priests, sisters, lay ministers, and seminarians of Trinidad-Tobago, West Indies.

We are also grateful to the many people who have shared their personal convictions and struggles around sexuality and relationships. Their commitment to carry their own stories with courage and grace have deeply moved and inspired us. Many of them have given us permission to quote from their experience. We have done so with reverence and gratitude — changing their names and identifying circumstances to honor their privacy.

With the first draft of this manuscript, we worked with a twenty-member advisory committee. This dedicated community of married and single people, sisters and priests, parents, educators, lay ministers and church leaders read our first drafts, attended all-day meetings on their own time, and offered honest feedback we trusted. Their generous gift of time and insight helped give direction to this book. To each of them, we extend our deep appreciation.

We have also been blessed with ongoing suggestions, clerical support, editing assistance, and warm times of friendship from our own closest communities of staff, friends and colleagues in Seattle. We especially want to thank Virginia Forte, Judy Knight, Sheila Barnes; our colleagues in the School of Theology and Ministry at Seattle University and our "Canoe Group."

There are no adequate words to express our appreciation to the Franciscan Sisters of Perpetual Adoration (FSPA), Fran's community, for the many ways they have supported this endeavor. Along with a generous financial grant, they have remained in the background, patiently nurturing this project. In many ways, this book belongs to them.

We also want to acknowledge Dorian Gossy,

whose expert editing skills fine-tuned this manuscript, while her sensitivity to an inclusive readership made it more accessible. We will always be grateful for her affirming words, wise suggestions, and playful sense of humor.

We met Roy M. Carlisle, Senior Editor, The Crossroad Publishing Company, after our initial manuscript was deemed too long. He has taken us on the "editorial ride" of our lives — cutting whole chapters (to be used in a later volume), shortening remaining ones, and changing the style of this book to a new, user-friendly format. Throughout the process, Roy has been as caring and kind as he was "surgical." We immediately connected with him and trusted his instincts, even though some of his suggestions were difficult. In the end, we have become friends and colleagues.

Finally, we want to express our loving appreciation to Dr. Gwendolin Herder, Publisher and CEO of The Crossroad Publishing Company, for her personal encouragement and affirmation, and her expert guidance in helping us focus this manuscript. We were impressed by her intuitive understanding of the message we were attempting to convey and deeply touched by her commitment to the vision we shared. To Gwendolin, and all the wonderfully supportive staff at Crossroad, we feel blessed that our paths have crossed.

About the Authors

FRAN FERDER

Fran Ferder is the co-director of Therapy and Renewal Associates (TARA), a ministerial counseling and consultation center in Seattle. She is a licensed clinical psychologist in Washington and Oregon and a part-time faculty member in the School of Theology and Ministry at Seattle University.

Fran is a native of Salem, Oregon, and a member of the Franciscan Sisters of Perpetual Adoration. She has had more than twenty years of ministerial and professional experience as a college professor, director of student counseling, psychotherapist, psychological consultant for various religious communities and dioceses, and a research director for a major social ministry study. Fran holds a Ph.D. in clinical psychology from Loyola University, Chicago, and a doctorate in ministry from Aquinas Institute of Theology, St. Louis.

Fran is also a frequent presenter at national conferences and workshops. She is author of *Words Made Flesh* (Ave Maria Press). She has published several articles in various journals over the past fifteen years. Her most recent is a chapter entitled "Qualities and Competencies of the Catechetical Leader" in *Empowering Catechetical Leaders,* published by the National Catholic Educational Association. Fran has co-authored (with Rev. John Heagle) *Partnership: Women and Men in Ministry* and *Your Sexual Self: Pathway to Authentic Intimacy.* Fran resides in Seattle, Washington.

JOHN L. HEAGLE

John Heagle is the co-founder and co-director of Therapy and Renewal Associates (TARA), a counseling and consultation center in Seattle. Since 1985 he has served as a licensed psychotherapist in the State of Washington and an adjunct faculty member in the School of Theology and Ministry at Seattle University.

Ordained a Catholic priest for the Diocese of La Crosse, Wisconsin, in 1965, John has had more than thirty-seven years of pastoral experience, including college teaching, campus ministry, justice and peace leadership, and ten years as a pastor. He holds an M.A. in philosophy from the Catholic University of America and a licentiate in canon law from the Pontifical Lateran University in Rome.

For the past seventeen years he has also served as a counselor, retreat director, and a presenter at national and international conferences and workshops. He is the author of seven books, including *Life to the Full, On the Way, Suffering and Evil,* and *Jesus: Divine and Human.* He is the co-author (with Fran Ferder, FSPA) of *Partnership: Women and Men in Ministry,* and *Your Sexual Self: Pathway to Authentic Intimacy.* John resides in Seattle, Washington.

crossroad

Of related interest

Carolyn Gratton
THE ART OF SPIRITUAL GUIDANCE

"What is most helpful about Carolyn Gratton's vision of spiritual guidance is that she places it in the context of all of life . . . a comprehensive vision that is integrative and practical . . . exciting and enabling. It will be of enormous help to all who aspire to become 'wise fish' "

–*Spiritual Book News*

0-8245-1223-5; $24.95 paperback

Peter M. Kalellis, Ph.D.
RESTORING RELATIONSHIPS
Five Things to Try Before You Say Goodbye

This fascinating book promises to restore broken or fragmented relationships. It offers concrete ways to put five important principles into practice so that any relationship may grow and regain peace and productivity.

0-8245-1880-2; $16.95 paperback

Peter M. Kalellis, Ph.D.
RESTORING YOUR SELF
Five Ways to a Healthier, Happier, and Creative Life

Kalellis's five-step plan puts readers in touch with the portrait of their restored self, dispelling harmful romanticism. The five steps are: acknowledging that you're not alone; restoring self-expression; undertaking honest self-evaluation; accepting your Self unconditionally; and finding your way from saturated existence to sacred reality.

0-8245-1934-5; $16.95 paperback

Of related interest by
RONALD ROLHEISER

AGAINST AN INFINITE HORIZON
The Finger of God in Our Everyday Lives

"A felicitous blend of scriptural reflection, shrewd psychological observations, and generous portions of letters sent to Rolheiser and his responses." –*Commonweal*

0-1965-5; $16.95 paperback

THE SHATTERED LANTERN
Rediscovering a Felt Presence of God

"Whenever I see Ron Rolheiser's name on a book, I know that it will be an amazing combination of true orthodoxy and revolutionary insight — and written in a clear and readable style. He knows the spiritual terrain like few others, and you will be profoundly illuminated by this lantern. Read and be astonished."

–Richard Rohr, O.F.M., Center for Action and Contemplation, Albuquerque, New Mexico

0-8245-1884-5; $14.95 paperback